MAIL FOR MIKEY

In 1971, Orson Bean wrote *ME AND THE ORGONE* about his search for sexual fulfillment in Wilhelm Reich's controversial form of psychotherapy. It was published and re-published, continued to sell and remains in print to this day.

MAIL FOR MIKEY

AN ODD SORT OF RECOVERY MEMOIR

ORSON BEAN

FORT LEE, NEW JERSEY

Published by Barricade Books Inc.
185 Bridge Plaza North
Suite 308-A
Fort Lee, NJ 07024

www.barricadebooks.com

Library of Congress Cataloging-in-Publication Data
A copy of this title's Library of Congress Cataloging-in-Publication Data is available on request from the Library of Congress.

ISBN 13: 978-1-56980-350-9

10 9 8 7 6 5 4 3 2 1

Manufactured in the United States of America

FOR ALLEY AND FOR VICTOR WOLFENSTEIN,
WHO HELPED US SO MUCH

Some years ago, I found myself sponsoring a young man in a twelve-step program. For some curious reason, I began keeping a log of the advice I gave him. Even more curiously, the log started to take on the voice of a fictional character: that of a retired marine. Perhaps it was easier for me to put down my thoughts as another character. I am an actor, after all. And I had served overseas for a year in the army, so I knew something about the military life.

I wrote a few chapters, then couldn't think of anything more to say. So I stuck the pages away in a drawer. Years went by. A lot of changes came down in my life. I became a Christian. One day, I stumbled across the discarded chapters, and it occurred to me how to turn them into a book. My imaginary marine began his mentoring again.

Mary Chase was asked once about her experience writing the great play, *Harvey*. "I didn't write *Harvey*," she said. "God did. I could hardly keep up with the pencil." In my case, the pencil went a little nuts.

This is, to be sure, an odd sort of memoir. I am a Christian working in what is widely perceived as an atheistic business. But is it? Not long ago, I was guesting on a TV show. Between takes, I sat in my canvas chair, reading a copy of C. S. Lewis' great book, *Mere Christianity*. I can't tell you how many people, crew and actors alike, came over to ask me about it. There seems to be a hunger out there, even in the television business.

I didn't want a Christian house to publish my little book. What I've written is aimed at folks who are interested, but suspicious. They keep sniffing around, but are terrified of becoming Ned Flanders. To my surprise and delight, Barricade Books (probably the antithesis of a Christian publishing house) took Mikey on. I hope you enjoy him.

Orson Bean
Venice, California

SENT: Tuesday, May 7, 1991 11:52 AM
To: mailformikey@aol.com
Subject: Your sponsor?

How the hell did I ever let this happen? Why did I buy a computer? No one else I know has one. Except you. Alright. Belief in coincidence is a form of superstition. You're in San Diego, I'm in Santa Monica, and I made your dad a promise. So I'll have to be your sponsor this way. If I can figure out how to make the damn thing work. You seem to know how to use it. I'm learning.

Mikey, listen to me. When you were up here for a minute last week and I said I'd consider this dumb arrangement, you kept bitching about the God thing, as you so delicately put it. About the people in the program who are trying to lay a spiritual trip on you. What can I tell you, Mikey? The God thing is not a problem unless you decide it is. Nothing is. People who decide their health is a problem get sick. The ones who decide dough is a problem are always broke. John Paul Getty used to carry his lunch to work in a paper bag. The richest guy in the world complained about the prices in the cafeteria. And it was his company.

You meet people out here in California, they've decided that what they eat is a problem. You see them in the health food stores. Gimmie some of them figs. And a pound and a half of prunes. They are the worst looking people you ever saw. The only worse looking ones are the guys selling them the stuff.

You joined the program because you couldn't stop drinking, right? You tried everything else, and it didn't work, right? So, you're twenty-one now. Or twenty, I guess. Your father told me you started when you were fourteen! So the program says you've got to admit you're powerless and turn the problem over to a higher power. You don't have to call it God, Mikey. You can call it a telephone pole if you want. Oh mighty telephone pole, relieve me of this compulsion to drink. What do you care if it's God or not? All you care is if it works. If it works, call it whatever you want. You don't have to believe in it, you just have to do it and see. You don't have to believe the TV is going to come on when you push the button, do you? You just have to push it and see what happens. If the show comes on, you watch it. If it doesn't, you read a book. Don't make a whole thing out of it. It's no big deal.

I was in Maxwell's this morning, that little ham-and-egg joint I took you to. On Washington. I'm with a guy I know who was in the corps with me. He knew your dad too. He's got twelve years clean and sober. I tell him about our arrangement, how I'm trying to sponsor you over the Internet. Oh, he says, yeah, I've heard of that. Alright, try it and see if it works, it's a new day and age. I'm sitting there listening to him over my Cream of Wheat. They don't have any oatmeal that day so I'm eating Cream of Wheat. The worst.

My grandfather back in Trenton used to make oatmeal and keep it in a big pot on the wood-burning stove for days. By day three, he'd say it really had some taste. He'd cut dates into it, and every day the dates would dissolve a little more and flavor the whole oatmeal. Delicious? And you'd crap like a gull. My grandpa took a dump morning and night for ninety-seven years. He claimed that was why he was never sick. I ought to write a book: "Crap Your Way to Health."

Anyway, back to the point. You don't have to believe in anything, Mikey. Don't even try. It just adds to the problem. Don't believe it, just do it. Get down on your knees in the morning and thank God for your night's sleep. Do it again at night and thank him for the day. It has nothing to do with religion. I think religion is a way of keeping God at a distance. It filters him through stained glass and organ music. It's like putting a cut in cocaine.

Mikey, do you want to be happy? It doesn't seem to mean much to a lot of people. Other things mean more. Like dough. Or success or security. But being happy always topped my list. That's why I drank. It's why I joined the Marines. Why I chased every good-looking babe I met. And it all worked for a while. But when it didn't, when my service career fell apart and the women left and the booze stopped working, I had to face it. I was screwed. There was nothing I could do to get happy. I gave up. And when I did, that's when God came into my life.

I can hear you saying yuck, God, goody-goody. I can see your face. Well, goody-goody is the last thing God is. If God is God, he's not just the God of sunsets and blue-birds, he's also the God of moose shtupping. That must be a majestic sight, Mikey. Short of a whale shtupp or an elephant shtupp, which God is also the God of, a moose shtupp must be a powerful spiritual experience.

Alright. Enough for now. Believe it or not, I have other stuff to do besides learnin' you about life. This house was built in 1925 and it's feeling its age. I've got a guy coming in at four to give me an estimate on new floors. It never ends. Since my discharge, I'm busier than when I was in uniform. The windows are next. I wanna get bigger ones to look out at the garden. Crazy old man and his flowers. I should be living in a bachelor pad like you. But I do love this joint. It's older than I am. Reminds me of my grandfather's place back in New Jersey.

I'll write you tomorrow, kid. Keep going to meetings.

SENT: Saturday, May 11, 1991 2:31 PM
To: mailformikey@aol.com
Subject: You went out.

Oh jeeze, Mikey. I just walked in and found your note. So, you really got smashed, huh? Well, at least you were whole-hearted about it. Thanks a bunch for the lurid details; more than I wanted to know. So you woke up at her place, and now she's off at work, and you have to decide if you're going to be back there when she gets home tonight with a nice little half gallon of Chablis and that beautiful body?

Mikey, you have to be strong. First with yourself, then with her. If you are, she'll respect your decision to lay off the booze. Women are into power. It's genetic. From the cave days. You have to let her know you mean it: you're through drinking, you can't handle it. If she thinks that's weak, to hell with her. You have to tell her you're on the program, Mikey. You're a drunk. That's the point. If you face it and make up your mind to change, she's going to see that as powerful.

There's a difference between people who don't want

13

to drink and the ones who want to and know they can't, Mikey. They're the kind of people you're going to meet if you stick with this program. They're the best. They've let a miracle come into their lives. They've given up and asked for help. And they've gotten it. People in the program don't say they're never going to drink again. They know better. They live one day at a time. They say, "With thy help, Lord, I won't take a drink today." Thy help. It's a show of respect. He likes to be praised. It's an eccentricity of his, Mikey. And when you get to know him, you feel like giving it to him.

You don't have to believe in God. You just have to ask for help whether you think there's anyone there or not. It works, Mikey. Just do it. We don't know how to run our lives. Drunks, I mean. We need a power greater than ourselves to take over. Look what you're doing. You're on the program a few weeks and you meet a girl and go out and get bombed again. I'm sure it was fun, Mikey. But why did you have to get drunk? I'll tell you why. Because you don't believe you would have been any fun sober. That's what I used to think. Dinner without wine? In a good restaurant? What the hell am I gonna drink? Iced tea, for God's sake? And never hanging out in bars anymore?

But I made friends on this program who are the best. Clean and sober and the best, Mikey. When God comes into your life, you don't turn into a goody-goody a babe like what's-her-face wouldn't want to shtupp. Kelly, you said her name was? That's just an excuse. Your ego doesn't want you turning your life over to a higher power. He wants to keep on running things even if it kills you. He's clever, Mikey, like the snake with the apple. He'll make you forget to go to a meeting. He'll convince you the dames will think you're a wuss if you order a 7-UP.

He's the damn devil, Mikey, your ego. He hates God because when you turn your life over to him, he's screwed. He loses his job. He's demoted to what he really is: an autonomic function like your taste buds or some damn thing. He's who got you drunk last night. And he's going to get you drunk again tonight if you listen to him. Maybe Kelly thought you were cute and adorable and tipsy and wanted to take you to bed. But if you keep it up, she's not going to think you're so cute in a few weeks when you throw up on her rug or something.

Look back, Mikey. Look back on every relationship you ever had when you were on the sauce. Didn't the dames all think you were terrific at first and wind up not being able to wait to get rid of you? Get your act together. You had a slip. It's not the end of the world. You don't want to start drinking again and have to hit a lower bottom than you hit. You're lucky. Maybe you needed this to learn something. Call and leave a message on her machine that you think she's swell, but you won't be able to see her tonight because you can't drink and you're going to a meeting. Tell Kelly you'll call in a few and take her out for coffee and explain who you are. If there's anything there for you, she'll understand. And like you better for it.

It's almost three, Mikey. Call work and tell them you'll be in tomorrow and it won't happen again. If they don't buy it, they don't buy it. Your only hope is to be completely honest with them. They know your act by now. You can't lie to them. If they've been putting up with you this long, it's because they like you and hope you'll stop trying to con them. I'll write you tomorrow, kid. Keep going to meetings.

Got your latest, kid. Glad you're hanging in there. Proud of you about Kelly. She seems to have taken it OK. Give it a few more days before you call her again. Aside from anything else, it's a good tactic. There's no greater aphrodisiac than indifference.

I'm beginning to get the hang of the damn computer. It sits there staring. "Use me. Use me." Alright, here goes. I never told you about my daughter, Mikey. I have a grown daughter. She's twenty-eight now. Lives in Qatar. It's a sheikdom in the desert somewhere. She's married to a guy who works for Standard Oil or something. A city planner. He designs playgrounds and parks and stuff for the Qatar government. Anyway, I don't see her very much. We used to be close as hell. Her mother died when she was little, and I got myself transferred stateside so we could be together. She was my kid with my first wife. My second wife is the one who ran off with the classical musician. She had a thing for bassoon players.

She kept shtupping bassoon players. It would have been bad enough if she ran off with a rock musician, but a damn bassoon player!

So my daughter and I had a special bond, see? A guy and his daughter with no mother in the house will develop that. I was stationed in Virginia and from when she was twelve, she kept house for her papa. That's what she called me. I thought we'd always be close. I mean, we could tell each other everything. Even after I got married again. Things were special between me and my daughter. Carmen. Her mother was Cuban. It was from when I was stationed at Guantanamo. What a story. I'll tell you sometime. Oh God, Carmen is gorgeous. Like her mama. Only she's a real mixture of the two of us. She's got shiny black Latin hair and freckles. A beautiful mutt. The white supremacist loonies complain about the mongrelization of the races. But mongrels are the most beautiful things on earth. Like those half-French, half-Vietnamese girls I used to lust after in Saigon. And a dame I knew who had Black, Oriental and Caucasian blood in her. What cheekbones. And she carried herself like a queen.

Mongrels are the best, Mikey. The strongest. The smartest. And the most beautiful. That goes for people and for dogs, too. Being in the corps, I could never keep a dog. But if I could have, I would have wanted one of those bastard part-Shepherds. You see them sometimes, four or five of them, running in a pack in a neighborhood somewhere. Maybe a couple of them have red bandanas tied around their necks. And they're going someplace, like boys heading for a sandlot. They're grinning, with their tongues hanging out. They stop every once in a while to sniff each other's butts, like they're checking to make sure it's still them. When I was a little kid, my grandpa told me why dogs do that. He said that once upon a time the dogs had a convention. Every dog in the world came to a big meeting at the Madison Square Garden. And they all hung their butts in the cloakroom. And right in the middle of the convention, when the head dog was giving his speech, somebody yelled fire. The dogs ran like hell, and they all grabbed the wrong butt. And to this day they're looking for their own.

Anyway, Mikey, I like mutts. Mutt dogs, mutt people and America, a mutt country. If there was a national dog of the USA, it would be one of those afternoon part-Shepherds with a red bandana around his neck. And I love my beautiful mutt daughter, Carmen. She got married to an Armenian guy from Massachusetts with a honk on him you could plow cornfields with. I mean, he's really nice, I like him. But when he and Carmen get around to having kids, if they've got their father's honk with their mother's freckles on it, that's going to be a sight to see.

Well, by the time I mustered out of the corps, Carmen had taken up with Vascan. Vascan Toomajanian. An Armenian city planner, what the hell do I know. Actually, he's pretty good at it. He turns out all this modern stuff. Stainless steel in the desert. Arches and fountains and parks, with places for camels to crap off to the side, probably, I don't know. Anyway she moves to Qatar. So we correspond. And she tells me everything, like she always has. When she's having trouble with her husband. Or how she can't stand some of the other wives. Or how the Arabs are driving her nuts. She's funny about it, but she bares her soul to me.

Then, all of a sudden she isn't writing so much. I keep writing her, but I only hear back once in a while. I ask her about it in my letters, and when she does write back, she says she's sorry, she's been so busy and all. But Mikey, it doesn't ring true. And then I find out she had a trip back to the states with Toomajanian for a week or so, and she never even called me. I mean, she was on the east coast in New York on his business and then up in Watertown to visit his folks. And I only hear about it after the fact from a friend of hers whose wedding she managed to get to while she was in Boston. The friend is passing through L.A. and calls me to say hi and mentions it. Not knowing I didn't know.

Well I'm devastated, Mikey. Heartbroken. And confused. I don't know what hit me. What did I do to her, I'm asking myself? I mean, I know I acted like a jerk a lot with the drinking and the broads after the bassoon shtupper left, but Carmen always seemed to love me anyway.

So, I figure I must have done something bad to hurt her, maybe when she was a kid, and it just popped into her mind now. And that's why she needs to hurt me back.

I write her a letter, Mikey, apologizing for whatever I must have done and asking her to forgive me. When she gets it, she's upset, and she calls me from Qatar. You can call anywhere from anywhere now. By satellite. There must be an elephant's graveyard of old satellites in orbit out there in space. Every time the batteries give out on one, they send up another and leave the dead one flying around where it is. If aliens ever do come visit us, they're going to have to travel through a crappy neighborhood before they set down on the planet, just like we do when we ride the bus into the city from an airport.

No, no, says Carmen on the phone. You didn't do anything to me, papa. I love you. It's just that I had a limited time in the States, and you were out in California. But papa, I love you, she says. And that's it. So I just settle in to a kind of disappointed funk, Mikey. Figuring my relationship with her won't ever be very close again, and I'll never know why.

I finally do get a chance to see her a year later when she and her husband plan to spend a week in England, and I suggest I fly over to meet up with them. We have an evening together. Her and Vascan and me at a restaurant in London, and she gets hostile with me. Making fun of my program, which I've written her about, asking for descriptions of the meetings, and then saying it sounds like EST or some damn thing. I let it pass, not picking up her bait. But I really feel lousy.

The next morning I call her at the hotel and say I'd like to see her alone, I want to talk to her. She says OK, and we make a date to go for a walk and then have dinner. Vascan is at a city planners' convention or something and busy anyway. I tell her on the phone I need for us to try to get the crap that's between us out of the way. And for the first time, she doesn't deny there is crap there.

So we arrange to meet at five in the afternoon in one of those beautiful little parks in London, Mikey. It's in front of her hotel. You can walk across the whole of London and never be out of a park. Some non-Armenian city planner designed it that way in 1611 during the reign of King Horsepucky the Third or something. It's an unbelievably beautiful city.

I get there a little early, and I'm sitting on a park bench watching the parade go by. There are these traditional English businessmen. Young guys, but they look exactly the way they're going to look when they turn fifty. Bowler hat, morning coat, striped trousers and rolled umbrella. And then there are these freaks from the moon with spiked green hair and their Vampira girlfriends. And they're all going to the same costume party dressed as different characters, Mikey, only they don't know it. And if any of them noticed me, which they didn't, I'm sure they would've thought I was the weirdo.

An English nanny goes by, pushing a pram that could've had a baby Prince of Wales in it. She's holding a little Christopher Robin boy by the hand and pushing the pram with her other hand. The little boy looks adorable, and I wonder which of the two types I've been watching he'll grow up to be: the businessman or the rebel? He's about six years old, and he's got on gray short pants and a blazer and a cap with an insignia on it.

He's got the hand that isn't in the nanny's stuffed down his pants, Mikey. I suppose he's holding on to himself the way little kids will do, all innocent. And I guess the nanny notices it the same time I do, or else she notices me noticing it and feels she ought to say something. So she looks down at the kid and says, in a perfectly sweet voice, don't touch your nasty, dear, there's a good boy.

After a while, my beautiful Carmen comes out of the hotel. I can see guys turning to look at her when she crosses the street. The English doorman and all. It's a strange feeling. My little girl is a sexy woman. She gives me a hug, but I can tell she's uptight. I know I am. Then we go for a walk in that English park, Mikey. If you have to get some talking done, there's no better place in the world to do it than one of those perfectly kept up English parks. All during the war, when Hitler's buzz bombs were smashing neighborhoods into the ground at night, the guys with the park commission caps would be out in the morning clipping the grass and tending the flowers because the agreement with King Horsepucky said they'd mow the lawn every day.

So I start things off, saying I love her and I don't care about the past except if it interferes with the present. And I want us to say whatever needs to be said, so we can be close again. And she starts to cry, Mikey. Thank God no English people are around just then to see it. Tears are rolling down her beautiful cheeks over her freckles. And the nub of what she says is she had a lot of growing up to do, and she did it late. After she got married. She had to deal with feelings that she might have dealt with when she was a teenager. But with her mom dead and her having to run the family, she felt she always had to put on a good front, even when I acted like a jerk. Always having to seem OK even when she wasn't. She loved our life together back then, she says. But there were things she just didn't deal with and she's having to deal with them now.

She looks at me and says what I need from you, papa, is for you to know I love you without my having to show it. I do love you with all my heart, but I can't really do much about it these days, and I'm not sure why. So I need you to just know it. Even if I act indifferent to you and don't write. Even if I'm critical and distant. Sometimes even nasty like I was last night. That's what I need from you right now, papa, if you can give it to me.

She stands there in the park with the tears on her beautiful face and something in me just melts, Mikey. I understand exactly what she means, and I want to give it to her. It's something no one else in the world can give her. Something really special that she needs a lot. I take her in my arms and hug her for a long time. Thank God there aren't any English people going by to see it. And I say OK, babe. That's all I needed to hear. You got it. I just let go of all my hurt pride and feel like her daddy again, even though she's a grown-up married woman. The bad feelings seem to fall away from her, too, Mikey. And the next few days we have in London are wonderful. Toomajanian is busy planning oases, and we get to spend a lot of time together. We never talk about what we said again. We don't have to.

Carmen still doesn't write much. My hunch is when she has a kid that will change. But even if it doesn't, that's OK. I write her without expecting an answer. Writing letters is more fun than getting them, anyway. The reason I went into this endless story is maybe Kelly needs something like that from you. Whether she does or not, maybe that's what you need to give her. I really grew from understanding what Carmen needed. And from being able to give it to her.

Mikey, I think all dames these days are going through something like that. It's hard for them, what with everything that's come down. The pill and the sex revolution and Women's Lib and all. It was probably cozy in the old days when we were holding doors for them. But I guess they were mad about it, too. And now they have to deal with all the feelings they stuffed. We can't understand them, and I think it's dumb to try. What we can do is learn to love them anyway. Without getting a lot back. Because God knows they can't love us much these days, with their careers and their yoga classes and their damn body building to show us how tough they are.

But I'm telling you, Mikey, if we can love them without getting much back till they're ready to give it, we'll learn a lesson. One you can maybe use with Kelly. Anyway, what the hell can we do? We're trained to try and please them. What was it Gallagher used to say? If your wife leaves you for another woman, should you hold the door for both of them? OK, I'll get back to you, kid. Keep going to meetings.

Mikey, will I ever learn to use this damn thing? I just erased half of what I'd written and had to start over. It's a curse. I've got a three bedroom house, two of which I don't need, and the only room it works in is the one where I sleep. I had to move the four poster upstairs and turn my bedroom into an office. Hal the computer is running my life.

Alright. In answer to your query, of course, I didn't always believe in God. For most of my life. It changed when I got on the program. Not right away, of course. The first few months, I mumbled higher power, higher power like everybody else. It could be a doorknob, the ocean, whatever. Sure, there were guys saying it was God, like they are to you, but I didn't pay much attention. Things were working for me just the way they were, and I didn't want to complicate the deal with any religious crap. But there was this one guy I heard speak. I heard him a few times, and he always impressed the hell out of me. Bobby was his name. That's how he'd always introduce himself, and we'd yell back hi Bobby. You know the routine.

This guy Bobby was one tough bugger, Mikey. Scars and tattoos. He'd done time in the pen. Hard time. The last time he was arrested, he was taken off the roof of a building in downtown L.A. by a SWAT team. Helicopters, the whole shebang. They sent him away for fifteen years for something pretty violent, I'm sure. He didn't say. It was his third conviction, but this was before three strikes so he didn't get life.

Well, while he's up the river, he starts going to meetings. To break up the monotony, I suppose. And somehow or other, he gets the message, and his whole life changes. While he's still there in the jug. He begins helping other cons and staying out of trouble, and they knock some time off of his sentence. By the time I run across him, he's out, of course, and working at a regular job, going to meetings and sponsoring a number of young guys, like I do you. My babies, he calls them.

If you ever want to see inner peace on somebody's face, Mikey, this guy's mug is the one to look at. Rough on the outside, but his eyes filled with the Holy Spirit. The third time I hear him speak is at that hall in Culver City, where they have meetings in the morning and at noon and at night, too. It's the noon one. On a Saturday. I want to talk to him after the meeting. He's standing on the sidewalk in front of the hall, and some cute young thing is bending his ear. There are a few of us hanging around, wanting to talk to him, but of course, we all understand that if a good-looking girl is praising him, probably flirting with him, good manners and common sense dictate we wait our turns.

The girl finishes and starts to leave, but before any of us can get a shot at him, something strange happens, Mikey. An L.A.P.D. motorcycle cop speeds by on his big, black Harley, spots Bobby, jams on the brakes, jumps off the bike, runs over and grabs hold of him. Holy God, we all think, he's done something bad again, and they've come to get him. But instead of arresting him, the cop gives him a big hug. Then he gets back on the Harley and blasts off. Bobby turns to the little group of us there on the sidewalk. One of my babies, he explains, and starts off down the street.

I decide to be a pain in the neck and hustle on after him. I catch up and introduce myself. I tell him about my years in the corps and how I've got a few months clean and sober and about my reluctance to think about my higher power as God. What advice does he have, I ask?

Get down on your knees, he tells me, and thank God every morning. Do it again at night. (It's what I've said to you, Mikey. That's where I got it.) But I don't think I believe in God, I say to him. It doesn't matter, he says, just do it. Why do I have to get on my knees, I ask him? He likes it, says Bobby. And that's all he says to me. He stands there looking at me for a minute, and then I say OK and thank him, and he takes off.

I'm staying, in those days, in a one-room joint with a Murphy bed, down on Fairfax. That night, when it's time for me to go to sleep, I get down on my knees beside the Murphy bed, feeling like a complete fool, and speak out loud. If there's anybody there, I say, thank you for the day. I've finally decided, I suppose, that since all else has failed, I'll follow the instructions. That night, I sleep like a log, and in the morning, I get down on my knees again and say if there's anybody there, thank you for my night's sleep.

I keep doing this, Mikey, day after day, and without my even being aware of it, it stops feeling foolish to me. It starts feeling good, in fact. After a while, I begin to feel as if my prayers are being heard. I don't know by who or what, but it's a good feeling. Then, before I know it, I feel as if there's something or someone there who knows me and cares about me. Actually loves me. My life starts getting better, Mikey. I just feel happier. Alright, I tell myself, I'll call it God. Thank you, God, I say. And I mean it.

That's how it began for me, and it's kept on getting better ever since. And I've started trying to help some other guys, the way I do you, and that makes me feel better, too. None of it makes any sense, but I don't care anymore. I just care that I'm happy. Happier than I've ever been.

A week ago, Mikey, I read a story in the paper. In the science section. The ratfinks who do experiments on monkeys, it says, find a pleasure center in the monkeys' brains. They stick a wire in there and give it a little electrical charge, and the monkey likes it. He likes it so much, he'll go without food to have it. There's monkeys have starved themselves to death to keep that thing turned on. Now, I say to hell with all guys who stick electrodes in chimps. There's nothing we can learn that's worth that.

But the experiment reminds me of how I feel about God. After a taste of his love, I want it more than anything. It's hard to describe. You know how you feel when you're in love with a dame? I mean head over heels? Well, it's more than that, because with the dame you're always a little nervous. She can change her mind. I mean, anyone who loves you can turn around and hate you. Alright, maybe not your mother, if you're lucky enough to have a mother who loves you. But even your mother is going to die, Mikey. And when that happens, she won't be loving you anymore. But God's love is never going to end. Even when you croak. Not that I'm in any hurry to go. I want to live long enough to tape a yogurt commercial. Ex-Marine, a hundred and six, rides a horse every morning. Recently took his eighth bride and eats two pints of Dannon yogurt a day.

It fills me with bliss, Mikey. It's like sneezing and laughing and eating angel cake all at the same time. Except you can't keep doing that. But God's love doesn't stop. Of course, I don't feel it all the time. After a while, my ego starts raising hell. He doesn't like it if I turn things over to God. It cuts back on his gig. He wants to be in charge. Like a bouncer in front of a disco. Or the doorman at a fancy hotel. When I was a little kid, my father took me to New York, one time. We walked past the Waldorf-Astoria on Park Avenue, and there he was: the doorman. Gold buttons, a big moustache and a top hat. And I said to my old man, does that guy own the hotel? My father laughed. He said it sure looks that way, doesn't it, kiddo.

When my ego starts taking over, I hit my knees and pray. I say, Lord, I love you, and I know you love me. And I need to feel it. Please quiet my head, God. Turn off the roof chatter that's driving me nuts. And after a while he does, Mikey. Sometimes right away. I start grinning and feel so damn grateful, I can't think of enough ways to thank him. And I don't want it to stop. I'm like that monkey with the wire.

My ego is the bouncer in front of God's disco. When I'm thinking straight, I walk right past him. Hey pal, how's it hangin' tonight, the wife and kids OK? Maybe I slip him a twenty. That's part of the game, Mikey. My ego's only human. He has his own funny little needs, and it doesn't hurt to lay something on him once in a while. He is what he is, and his job is not all that great.

Long hours dealing with a lot of crap.

You know something I've noticed, Mikey, apropos of nothing and out of left field? Cripples seem happy. Deformed people. Gimps of all kinds. When they get past the hurt and rage and accept that they ain't one of the Beautiful People and the bouncer is never going to let them in the disco, poof! Suddenly they're in. Our egos keep us from seeing the truth, and a poor gimp hasn't got much of an ego.

When I can let go of my ego, Mikey, I see what I really am: God's kid that he loves. And I see gimps who have that. They've stopped trying because they know it's hopeless. I'm not saying you shouldn't try. You can't learn to stop trying til you've tried and tried. It's all part of God's game plan. He could have created us all perfect, knowing who he is and who we are. Then we'd just be blissed out all the time. Instead he zaps us with amnesia. Then he drops some hints about the truth. If we're greedy enough to be happy, sooner or later, we'll figure out the game plan.

The old Greek legends are full of labors and tasks, Mikey. Ulysses has to perform all kinds of impossible stuff to get back home. Home is with God. It's being in touch with who we really are. Everything is so damn different from what it seems, Mikey. And that's part of the game. God loves it when we beat the scam, figure out what he did to us and find a way to steal home. He loves us unconditionally, but we have to earn the right to know that.

It's so hard for me to explain this stuff to you, Mikey. I don't even get it myself. My mind is a two-transistor radio, and God is a classical music broadcast. Live from the Met. I can tune in the station and get a hint of his power on my little four-buck made-in-Taiwan radio. Later, I save up and buy a thousand bucks worth of hi fi equipment. Now I hear the broadcast a whole different way. More information is coming through, Mikey. Then one day maybe I get rich. I fly to New York, wrangle a ticket and there I am in the tenth row at Lincoln Center. The Philharmonic is playing Mozart. That's the presence of God, Mikey. Right now my mind is a Radio Shack two transistor. I only have a clue, but it's enough to thrill me.

Don't worry, I'm not going to become a fanatic, Mikey. I'm not running off to live in a cave in Tibet. I can be as connected to God here in my kitchen as I can on top of Mount Everest. Or at the flicks or the Burger King. I can learn to love him standing on line for a Whopper. But God makes it hard. Deliberately, I think. When I was a kid, I'd complain to my grandfather about something I had to do that was too hard, and he'd say if it was easy, everybody would do it; hard is what keeps out the riff-raff.

God makes us forget about him on purpose. We sense there's something terribly important we can't quite remember. We feel the loss and don't know what would fill it and make us whole. We try everything, Mikey: fame, power, sex, drugs, money. Or maybe rage or war. Sometimes we feel so hopeless and full of despair, we let ourselves go crazy. And some crazy people find God. They retreat into themselves. Give it all up. And there, right in front of them, is what they've been looking for. They think the only way they can have it is to stay nuts, so they won't come back. They just sit there in the corner, happy as clams, grinning to themselves.

Astronomers keep finding new stuff in the cosmos. It's never going to stop. They'll build bigger telescopes and find more galaxies until one day, some astronomer will say enough already, this is ridiculous. I'm not saying it isn't fun to look out there, to search the heavens. It's all fascinating stuff. Spiral nebulae and black holes and God knows what. Literally. But you won't find the meaning of life in the cosmos. It's all right here, Mikey. This instant. In you. In me. When you feel God's unconditional love, you understand the meaning of life.

Mikey, I don't know from religion. The truth is, most of it turns me off. It doesn't seem to have anything to do with God. Did you ever read the Bible? There were always Gideon Bibles in the cheap hotels I stayed in by the bus stations. The Bible is full of the wildest stuff in the world. Winged monsters with a lot of heads and fire shooting out of their butts. I guess the fundamentalists just have to buy into that stuff. Or maybe it's true, what do I know?

The Old Testament is full of stuff about guys shtupping their brothers' wives. And Lot's daughters getting him drunk and banging him. And Abraham letting the king of Egypt give his wife a pop and getting paid off in camels and slaves. Wild, hilarious, far-out stuff, Mikey.

I'm not knocking it. It's great Arabian Nights type stuff. But what does any of it have to do with God? My plan is to leave out the middleman and deal direct with the Maker for big savings. I don't want a watered-down God, filtered through laws and codes and legends. I want the real thing. I just love him so damn much. I'm so grateful he made me and stuck me in this light show to play. Religion is like the bottled-water industry, Mikey. God and water are free. What we pay for is the packaging.

We've got to keep an open mind about what reality is. Everything is so different from what it seems. Once you get in touch with God, all the "important" stuff turns trivial. Success and failure get turned upside down. If a gimp in a wheelchair is better off than a jet-setter, what does anything mean? Renounce worldly goods? Mikey, it seems to me that wherever we are is as good as any other place. Everyone is in the best seat. That's what some guy at a meeting said once. God is in us. Or we're in him. And when we start figuring out what's real and finding our way home, he helps us.

He talks to us if we let him. I ask him questions, and he

answers me. It's a real voice inside my head. Oh jeeze, Mikey, you're going to think I'm a whacko. Sometimes I'll just tell him I love him. And he'll say, I know you do, kid. That's all. If he tells me what to do, I do it. I've turned my life over to him, Mikey. I should have a sign: Under New Management. Of course, I still screw up. Just to keep the franchise. But I know I'm supposed to do God's will and not my own. What I want is my will. What I get is his will.

Ol' debil Ego whispers in my ear don't settle for what you get. Achieve! Take control! And it always sounds right, Mikey. My ego is so damn clever. He'll get me out of sync with what really makes me happy. Then, when I'm all screwed up, he whispers have a drink, snort a line, call a dame, let me help you. I've got good advice, and it's free. Well, it's not free, Mikey.

I know it feels wimpy. Always choosing what is. Where would Donald Trump be if he did that, right? Well, how do you know he wasn't listening to God himself? How do you know God didn't pull the Donald aside and say listen, Don, I want you to make a tower and shopping plaza on Fifth Avenue. I want you to decorate it with pink marble and put in a waterfall and a guy banging out show tunes on a Steinway. I want you to build a K-Mart for the rich. The thing is we don't know, Mikey. Trying to get it all to make sense is one of the ego's tricks. Endlessly questioning things keeps us from acting on them.

I drove up to Malibu the other day, and I'm sitting there on the beach watching the surfers check out the waves, waiting for just the right one like they do: not this one, not that one. And I start thinking about the waves. Each one has its own character. Maybe there's a perfect wave somewhere off the coast of Africa. But the one the surfers just passed on still has its own personality. It's unique. It's not like any other wave. I could give it a name. Mel. It's born. Now I see another one starting to pull together out past the surfers. A new young wave. The one called Mel is middle-aged now. Each separate wave has its own personality. It's born and lives; it gets old and dies. And the whole time, it's still part of the ocean.

But it forgets that, Mikey. It thinks it's just a wave. Maybe it's ambitious: hey, I'm the greatest, ride me, I'm perfect. Maybe it's a loser: aw hell, who'd want to surf me. Maybe it's a gentle wave: I'm beautiful. Little kids come splash in me; I won't toss you around. Every wave is different. Donald Trump is a tidal wave. A housewife in Chino is a soft gentle wave. They're both wonderful creations. Look. Mel just died. Funeral services for immediate family and friends only.

Mikey, you and I are waves. We're part of God's ocean, and we have a certain form for a while. Surfers will ride us or they won't. We'll wash seaweed up on the beach or we won't. We'll get created off the coast of Africa, or we'll live and die in Malibu. But the whole time, we're waves, Mikey, we're still part of the ocean. It's eternal so we are, too. God made us. God loves us. God wants us to figure out who we really are and find our way home to him. He keeps a light on in the window. He'll put up some coffee and make us a sandwich no matter how late we get there.

Okay, end of sermon. Hang in there, lad. Keep going to meetings.

I'm sitting at the computer in my former bedroom, and the warm California sun is shining through the window. Of course, it rained all weekend when people wanted to be out. Now it's Monday and beautiful. God's little prank to remind us who's in charge, I suppose. The spring flowers in my garden are mind-boggling. Here I am, a confirmed bachelor, and I've got an English country garden that a dame should be puttering in.

Speaking of dames, I'm sorry to hear it didn't work out with Kelly; glad to hear it's working out with Kiera. You do love your Ks, don't you. Jeeze, you work fast. Well, I guess you're irresistible, that's all there is to it. I hope you're being serious with this new one. You're twenty-one now, you shouldn't just be having play dates. Alright, alright. None of my business. As long as it doesn't interfere with your program.

Speaking of play dates, Mikey, here's what happened to me: it seems the dames abhor a vacuum. They can't stand to see a guy without a woman in his life. I run into

41

an old friend of the bassoon shtupper the other day. It turns out she's on the program now, and there she is at a meeting. She gives me a big hello and doesn't mention the shtupper, which is nice of her. She gabs with me for a while. This and that, I'm looking good, how long have I been on the program, am I seeing anyone? You know. Then she asks for my number. I figure she's going to make a move herself, she's giving me a big smile and all. But when she calls, it's about another dame.

I mentioned you to a gal I know, she tells me. Right away I'm on orange alert, Mikey. I'm not too crazy about gal. The dames should be called women. Or if you like, dames or some other form of endearment. But gal is when you want to say girl, but the dame is too long in the tooth. Gals wear hair spray and write their appointments down in Today-at-a-Glance books. They don't have a man in their life, and they want one.

This gal is on the program, the shtupper's friend says, and she knows who you are. She's been at some of the same meetings as you and heard you speak one time. She thinks you're very attractive. Oh God, Mikey, my mind starts racing. Part of me remembers the good times. Being in bed with a lady I love and the two of us curling up and sleeping like spoons. And of course, my head immediately jumps to a romantic conclusion to this date. But the realistic part of me says schmuck, a blind date at your age? You're OK the way you are. Don't rock the boat.

I can't get it together to say no, Mikey, so I take the dame's number and call her. I get a machine, of course, and her voice sounds nice enough. Then she calls me back and gets my machine. This is starting to be the romance of the robots. Finally we connect. We blab at each other a while, and then I say, so if you're free one night this week, why don't we take in a flick and then grab a bite to eat?

That would be swell, she says. Any night is fine with me. This makes me nervous, Mikey. Over availability. But I say OK, how about tomorrow? I've got my paper in front of me on the kitchen counter opened to the movie section. I'm hoping she'll go for one of the pictures playing at the 14 Cinemas. It's in the outdoor shopping center at Century City. I hate most of that place, Mikey, Century City. But the section around the 14 Cinemas is great. Little outdoor spots to eat and hot dog carts and a good bookstore to browse in. People walk around there, Mikey, like in a small town. Most parts of L.A., nobody walks anywhere. People get in their cars to go to the bathroom.

So I read her the choices from the movie ad, and we pick one we both like. I live quite near Century City, she says. Why don't you come to my place and park here, and I'll drive us over to the theater? Oh God, Mikey, the Black Widow is sucking me into her trap. I say, awful casual, the parking is so easy at the 14 Theaters, why don't we both drive there and meet by the box office? Oh alright, she says, and we agree on a time. It's the 5:30

show. She gets off work at five. I figure we'll catch the flick and then go eat in one of the restaurants in the mall there. That'll be from about 7:30 to 8:30, and we'll see what happens after. The reason I'm suggesting we start off with a movie is so I won't have to talk to her for the first two hours. I'm a wreck, Mikey. I haven't had a date in years.

The next afternoon I'm brushing my teeth and gargling with Scope and trying to decide what to wear. I flash on my first dates in Junior High back in Trenton. I always took a bath around five p.m., staying in the john forever, my folks banging on the door what the hell you doing in there? I'd use Five Day Deodorant pads and glop Wildroot Cream-Oil on my hair, every strand in place. I'd have a pack of Sen-Sen in one back pocket and a clean handkerchief in the other. A gentleman always carries a clean white handkerchief in case the lady needs it. I never understood why a lady would need a guy to carry a clean handkerchief for her. Was she going to hock a lunger in it and then fold it up and hand it back to him?

I plan on getting to the 14 Theaters in plenty of time so I'll be relaxed and casual, Mikey. But of course I fool around with one thing or another till I've got barely enough time to make it by 5:20, which is when we said we'll meet. I park my car in the underground garage and take the escalator up the two flights to the open air. Since I don't know what she looks like and she says she'll recognize me, we've left it she'll be the one to make the contact. It's like a spy thing from a bad miniseries.

As I come out the top of the escalator, there's a great-looking young babe standing there with a sensational body. She's wearing a safari outfit. Of course, my warped mind immediately says oh boy, it's her! Needless to say, she looks right through me, Mikey. She's waiting for some jock her own age. Well, that's my nature, amigo. I guess when I'm eighty-nine, I'll be looking at the young ones like my grandfather did.

I turn left out of the escalator and immediately run into an old dame with gray hair and a shopping bag. Oh God, it's her, my brain screams. I'm panicked, Mikey. What the hell am I going to do? But, of course, it isn't her, either. Why can't I just wait and see what happens? But no, I have to jump to conclusions. It's this gorgeous young one. It's that old one sporting the aluminum walker. I'm driving myself nuts, Mikey.

I move toward the ticket booth, and suddenly there she is. She spots me in the crowd, raises her hand and calls out hi. I give her a hi back and walk over. She's a good-looking dame, Mikey. Not the young lovely in the safari suit and not the old one with the shopping bag. But a good-looking one the right age for me. By that I mean about ten years younger. She's a classic Beverly Hills princess of the mature variety, Mikey. The blonde hair combed back tight with hair spray. The year-round tan and the nose job. No don't laugh, Mikey, she's attractive. A good-looking dame of a certain type. A nice figure, clothes from the Drive and a Gucci bag.

Of course, the committee in my head has not stopped just because I know who she is now. I'm taking her inventory like she was the family business. Well, I say, grabbing her by the elbow, let's pick up the tickets and head into the theater.

Is there any place around here that sells Tums, she asks, or Rolaids? How the hell do I know, Mikey? If she needed Rolaids, why didn't she bring them? Or maybe it was the sight of me that turned her stomach sour. No, she already knew who I was.

Jeeze, I'm not sure, I say. I know there's no drugstore around here or any other kind of place that sells Tums or Rolaids. From antacids, you can't make the kind of rent they charge in this neck of the woods. Well, we have a few minutes, we could look around, I tell her.

Oh no, she says. It's not important. I guess it's just that I ate junk food today and it doesn't agree with me. We're standing in line for the tickets now, Mikey. Junk food doesn't agree with her. God. We take the escalator up to the theater lobby. It's wonderful. I love it. The new neon version of the grand old movie palace. These exhibitors are smart, Mikey. The difference between renting a video and going out to the flicks is that the way the lobby looks can make it an event.

The guy takes our tickets, and we walk past the candy counter. The only thing I don't like about the 14 Theaters is they don't have Goobers. Raisinettes they got up the kazoo, but not a damn Goober in sight. What they do have is a separate refreshment counter with elegant stuff in it. Cappuccino and little brownies and things. For the fancy people. And at that counter, they sell Jordan Almonds. Not bad. The rich man's Goobers. It isn't that I'm hungry anyway, but it's nice to know they're there. A buck and a half. Or maybe it's a buck and a quarter. But the damn Goobers are a buck and a quarter at the movies these days, anyway.

When I was a kid, Mikey, everything was a nickel. The kids in my neighborhood went to the movies on Saturday morning. There was no TV. I used to tell Carmen that. Her mind couldn't grasp the concept. Life without electric lights she could get. Without blenders, hair dryers, anything. Even automobiles. Easy. She's crazy about horses. She'd love it if there weren't any cars. I tell her the streets would be filled with horse buns. So what, she says. She likes horse buns. Likes the smell. And likes to see the little birds picking seeds out of them.

Saturday morning at the movies was the highlight of my week, Mikey. Kids came from all over the place. I mean the far reaches of the neighborhood. I had a half-hour walk to get there, and there were kids who lived twice as far away as I did. The theater was always packed. I'd be half way there, and I'd see another kid hustling along, and I'd think what if he gets the last seat? And I'd start walking faster. Then two boys would come from another direction heading for the theater, and I'd start running. The kid I'd been walking faster than would spot me, and he'd start running too. Then the other two kids would try to catch up to us. As we got closer to the theater, there were crowds of boys running like crazy. Then we'd all arrive, and it was nothing. No big mob being turned away or anything. Just the usual line of kids waiting to get in.

And boys outside the theater yelling, I got six, who's got five? I got six, who's got five? It was a dime to get in to the movies then, Mikey. But every once in a while, the Muni, that was the theater, would have a one-cent sale. The second ticket was a penny if two kids came together. They didn't like you meeting up with strange kids and pooling six cents and five cents on the sidewalk there in front of the theater. The manager would come out and try to catch the kids who were doing that. You have to arrive together to take advantage of the one-cent sale, he'd yell. Why did he care, Mikey?

The candy was on special on sale days, too. The first package of Goobers or Walnettos or Milk Duds was a nickel and the second one a cent. Two kids would always come up with three cents apiece for that deal. The manager would watch for troublemakers. You, he'd say, pointing at a boy, usually a tough kid from North Tren-

ton. I know who you are. I'm watching you. He didn't
really know who he was, Mikey. He was full of it, like all
grownups. The worst thing the tough kids did was once in
a while they'd chip in to buy one kid a ticket. He'd go up
to the balcony and open one of the side fire doors, and
five or six of his friends would climb up the fire escape
and sneak in free. That was the extent of bad in those
days, Mikey. No drive-bys with Uzi machine guns.

When the show was over, Mikey, features only lasted
an hour and a quarter in those days, the theater would
empty out around noon. A hundred boys would race
across the square and descend on the Five and Ten to
shoplift. I'm not kidding. There were literally about a
hundred boys who'd move through the place like lo-
custs. The manager would stand at the door and yell,
I'm watching you, I'm watching you. But, of course, it
was hopeless. We'd go in through the front doors and
be out the back doors in about five minutes. A few kids
bought stuff I guess, but mostly it was theft. Toy soldiers,
Little Big Books, yo-yos. Whatever. A kid I knew named
Sharkey cut the pockets out of his knickers. He'd drop
stuff in there and fill the knickers and go out the door stiff
legged, he couldn't bend his knees, Mikey.

In those days, things at the Five And Ten actually cost
five cents and ten cents. A nickel was coin of the realm
in my childhood. Nobody ever saw a quarter. A dime
bought lunch. A grilled cheese sandwich was a nickel

at the drugstore counter, and the other nickel was for a Pepsi. No kid bought Coke because it was six ounces and Pepsi was twelve. I didn't understand why Coke was even manufactured. We'd sit at the counter and stretch the sandwich out as long as we could, reading comic books free from the magazine rack till the guy finally chased us out. Return deposit bottles were called glass nickels.

So at the 14 Theaters, my date and I are walking past the refreshment stand, and I ask if she requires any foodstuffs. Maybe something will take the place of the Tums or Rolaids. They have little cups of sorbet or some damn thing at the gourmet counter. It might soothe her stomach. She says not now, maybe later. And we move into the theater. It's one of the smaller theaters, Mikey, because the picture has been playing a while and it's on its last legs. Most of the theaters in the complex are big, and even this one has a fairly decent sized screen. I hate some of the little theaters in the malls around town. There's people I know have bigger screens on their TV at home. I don't want to pay to sit in a closet and watch a VCR. Halfway through the picture, she says excuse me and goes out to go to the john. When she comes back, she's got popcorn. I guess she's nervous, too.

When the movie is over, we take the escalator down to ground level. It's around 7:25 and still light out. I love the daylight savings time. Who needs that hour of sunlight in the morning? To hell with the farmers. They're screwed anyway, getting up at the crack of dawn to turn on the milking machine. I like the day to last longer at the end of it. I guess when I was drinking, I didn't mind short days. Happy Hour started earlier, and I didn't feel guilty about getting smashed at 4 p.m. if it was dark out already.

There's a Chinese restaurant I've never eaten in downstairs near the box office, and there's the Stage Deli across the way. I say why don't we look at the menu in the window of the Chinese joint and see if there's anything there that tickles our fancy? If there isn't, we could go to the Stage. She says, well, I like the Stage, do you like the Stage? I say sure I like the Stage. She says so why don't we go to the Stage?

For some reason, I feel manipulated in a subtle way, Mikey, as we sit down at our table in the Stage. Is it my male need to be in charge? We look at the four-page menu. It's too big for me. I don't like decisions. I like a menu with five or six things on it tops. Going to a restaurant should not be work. Making decisions is a pain in the neck, and there's enough of those I have to make in my life without being handed a menu the size of the Torah.

When I go in a Jewish restaurant, Mikey, I'm right away hungry for matzo ball soup. I must have been a Jew in past lives. This time around, I'm trapped in the body of an aging Gentile. I decide that what I'm going to have for dinner is a bowl of matzo ball soup. The truth is I was so nervous about the date, I've been eating all day. I've got a bag of Chicken Littles from the Colonel in my freezer, and I can pop one in the nuke and heat it up in thirty seconds. I guess I ate about four of those Chicken Littles that afternoon, so no wonder I'm not hungry. That's all you're going to have? says my date when she asks me and I tell her. You don't want at least a salad or something with it? No salad, I say. Hmm, she says, and studies the menu.

Why don't we split an appetizer, and then we'll both have soup, she says. You can order an appetizer if you want, I say. And if I like, I'll have a bite of it to keep you company. But basically, I'm just into having my matzo ball soup. I'll have some rye bread on the side. Hmm, she says, and looks at the menu some more. Well, maybe I'll just order a hamburger. A hamburger in a Jewish restaurant, Mikey? And what happened to the appetizer? Why is she trying to have a say in what I eat? And why do I give a damn if she is? Why am I obsessing about this? Why is the average rainfall in the Sudan the lowest in Africa? Why is the committee in my head unwilling to take a break for twenty seconds?

We eat our dinner. The matzo ball soup tastes like if Campbell's made a line of Jewish soups. The bread is Pepperidge Farm seeded rye. Oh well, it's L.A. They say a goy from New York is more Jewish than a Jew from Minneapolis. We make chitchat. Her ex-husband, her grown kids, what she does, I guess. I can't remember, Mikey. I'm trying to keep an open mind. I ask for the check. She goes to the john again. I tell her I'll meet her at the cashier.

We walk into the Farmers' Market building next door. There's a concession in the middle of it that sells fudge. The Fudge and Cappuccino it's called. Her eyes light up. We'll buy a bag of fudge and take it back to my place and sit and have a good time, she says, and walks over to the fudge counter.

My heart sinks, Mikey. I don't want the damn fudge. I don't want to go back to her place. I don't want to sit and have a good time. Why don't I just say so? I have looked men in the eye and shot them in two wars. Why am I letting this dame and her fudge become a problem for me? I walk up behind her. She turns around and gives me a dazzling smile. Do you like white chocolate, she asks? No, I say. Have you ever tried it? No. Then how do you know you don't like it? I never shtupped a moose, I know I don't like it, I answer. Hostile. God, I don't want to get hostile with her.

Listen, I say, the truth is, I don't want to go back to your place. I'm nervous. I won't relax there. What I'd like to do is walk around here. We could look in the windows of shops and browse in the bookstore. Then maybe we'll find a little outdoor café and have a cup of coffee. OK? You eat the fudge. I'll look for an ice cream place and buy a cone. Well alright, she says, managing not to look too hurt. But you could have one piece of the fudge.

I'm sure she's a nice dame. And if she had just let things be, just let whatever happened happen . . . Or if I could have been more laid back and not let her press my buttons. Well, we'll see. She was OK. At least she didn't ask if I had a clean white handkerchief.

Alright, nuff said. Keep going to meetings.

Wish you were going to be up here for the Fourth. Santa Monica does a grand show at the pier, around nine when it's really dark. Well, you're probably too grown-up for fireworks anyway.

It sounds like your new girl is the real thing. I can't wait to meet her. Maybe I'll have to take the train down there. I love that train to San Diego. Or maybe you can bring her up here. No hurry. Let it happen in its own time. The main thing is she seems fine with your being clean and sober.

Alright. My news. It appears I have a dog, Mikey. He's been coming around the last few days looking for food. Which, of course, I've been giving him. Scraps and bones and a plate of spaghetti. Dogs will eat anything. So today I went to Ralphs and laid in some Alpo. I tried all the usual ways to find out who might have lost him. Looking for lost dog signs on phone poles. Calling West L.A. Animal Services. I took him there to see if he had one of those implants with the owner's info, but he doesn't.

55

He's tame, Mikey. Friendly. He hops right in the Honda and rides like dogs do, hanging out the window, drinking up the breeze. So whoever he belonged to either doesn't want him or anyway isn't knocking himself out to find him. I guess he's mine.

He's one of those part-time shepherds I love, you know. I'll have to get him a red bandana when I'm sure I can keep him. I don't want to get my hopes up too high. I told you I never had a dog being in the corps and all. It's not completely true. When I was a kid, I had one. I was twelve or thirteen. Twelve, I guess. I'd been begging my dad. Can I have a dog? Can I have a dog? Finally he said yes, I could have a dog, a small one, but I had to feed it with my own money.

There was no such thing as an allowance back then, Mikey. I earned every cent I had. Shoveling snow in the winter and cutting grass in the summer. I washed windows, five cents a side. I'd drive my bike over to Gebbott's Bakery on Market Street and buy day-old éclairs. Actually, they were funny little things called Gebbott's Creme Friedcakes. I'd pick up a dozen, two for a nickel, and then peddle them door to door for a nickel each.

On Memorial Day, people went to the cemetery to leave flowers on the family graves. It was a long walk from the streetcar up the hill to the memorial park. I had a big wagon I filled with quart bottles of soda. I got them four cents a pop at the A and P. I'd have a big block of ice to chill the soda and stacks of paper cups. I got five cups out of a quart. That was twenty-one cents a bottle profit, less the cost of the ice and the cups. I'd haul the wagon up the hill and set myself up at the top near the cemetery gate. People were hot and thirsty after the long climb from the streetcar. I always sold out.

When lilacs were in season, they'd grow in vacant lots or in back of apartment houses. I'd lug a stepladder and cut dozens of lilacs and sell bunches of them in front of Pillato's Shoe Repair. Pillato never objected. I'd always save the last bunch for him to take home to Mrs. Pillato.

When I turned fifteen, I got a job after school washing dishes and helping out in the kitchen at Mr. Economy's cafeteria. Economy was a Greek. His real name was Economakis, but he changed it to Economy, he said, to sound more American. The cooks and helpers in the kitchen would yell and carry on in Greek. The pot washer was low man on the totem pole. He had it in for me because I was the only one under him. He'd make me scrub his dirty pots, but I never did it right. He donno nuttin! He donno nuttin! he'd yell. No one paid attention, but I can still hear him. He donno nuttin!

I took the number five bus to the Animal Rescue League building in Trenton, Mikey. I could hear dogs barking when I opened the door. I was twelve and nervous they wouldn't let me take a dog on my own. It wasn't a problem. They'd have been happy to let me have every dog in the place. There was a long hallway just inside the front door with double-stacked cages on both sides. Mutts were yapping. There'd be a small license fee, and that would be that. I started to look. It was heartbreaking, Mikey. These dogs so wanted to be adopted. In the last cage on the left, I saw him. A two-thirds grown part-shepherd. I touched the cage, and he licked my fingers through the wire mesh. I fell desperately in love.

He was too big, Mikey. I knew that's what my father would say. We can't keep an animal that size, he'll eat us out of house and home. I could hear his voice. But I had to have him. I signed the form and handed over the fee, I think it was a buck seventy-five, a good part of my savings. I hadn't thought about a leash, but one of the guys found a hunk of clothesline for me. He opened the cage, and the dog came out and licked my hand again. I was never so thrilled in my dozen years, Mikey.

The guy tied the rope around his neck, and we were out the door. There was no way I was going to take the bus home with him. I didn't know if they'd let him on, and what's more, I was afraid he'd freak out and run, and I wouldn't be strong enough to hold him. It took two hours to walk home with Buster. That's the name I picked for him along the way. He stopped to sniff at every hydrant, phone pole and bush. When cars honked, he'd shiver. I realized he was a skittish dog. Small wonder, I thought. Who knew what he'd been through to wind up in that cage. Well, never again. Buster was mine now, and he'd always be protected.

When we got home, I took a deep breath, climbed the three steps of the front stoop and opened the door. I could hear my father in the kitchen explaining something to my mother "for the umpteenth time." I lead Buster through the living room and into the kitchen. My father was standing in front of the new refrigerator. Until that year, we'd had an icebox. Once a week the iceman would deliver a big block of ice like the one I'd lugged to the cemetery and stick it in the top of the box. The cold air would move down through the insulated chest and cool the food. Underneath, a tray collected the water that dripped into it as the ice melted. It was always my job to empty the tray. I hated it because the water would slosh on me when I lifted it and wet the front of my pants. This was not a good look for a young boy.

Cripes, you call that a small dog? No way that thing is staying in this house. Get it out of here now! My father, of course. Now, George. My mother, as usual, had been into the cooking sherry. It's not going to cost us anything. I started to whimper. The drama went on for ten minutes, ending with an order for me to keep it out of the living room and don't let it bite anyone.

I was really happy, Mikey, for the first time in my life. But scared too, of course. I had something to lose now.

And lose him I well might with the parents I had. Keeping him out of their way became my number one job. It was summer. School was out. We walked the streets of the neighborhood. When we'd stop to watch a sandlot ball game and boys were screaming, he'd whimper and shake. He slept at the foot of my bed, and we'd gaze into each other's eyes for hours on end. I felt so much love. Two weeks went by. One day my father was off at work, and my mother was into her afternoon sherry, sitting at the kitchen table. Buster and I walked in looking for dog biscuits.

C'mere, doggie, she said. She was slurring, Mikey. Leave him alone, mom, I said. I knew Buster was nervous around her. Don't tell me what to do, she said. C'mere, mutt. She reached out and grabbed his clothesline. She pulled his muzzle close to her face and slobbered a boozy kiss on him. The poor thing whimpered and tried to pull away. Please mom, leave him alone, I begged. He doesn't like it. You respect your mother, damn you! C'mere dog. She pulled him to her. He tried to back off. She wrestled him closer. He whined, Mikey. Then he barked, and then, God help me, he nipped at her cheek. Ow, she shrieked! Ow ow! She let the poor dog go, and he ran to me. I told you, mom, I told you he didn't like it. I was terrified. Tears were rolling down my face. Get out. Get out. You and that damn dog. He bit me, damn you! We ran to our room.

My father came home from work that night. She told him what happened. Her version of the story. I said nothing, Mikey. I dreaded what I might hear. Five days went by. I stayed out of the house with the dog as much as possible. The fifth day was Saturday. My father was home from work. I was in my room trying to keep Buster out of his way. I could hear them whispering in the kitchen. Then he yelled come out here, I have something for you. I did as I was told. Here, he said, here's a nickel. Go down to the drugstore and drink a Pepsi there. It was unheard of, Mikey. My father had never given me a nickel in my life. That's OK, I said, I don't want a Pepsi. My father scowled. Do what I tell you. Take this nickel and go down to the corner. I'll go get Buster, I said. No, leave him. Here, take the nickel.

I was terrified, Mikey. I took the nickel and ran faster than I'd ever run to the drugstore, three blocks away. I swilled the drink and then sped home. As I turned the corner of our street, a Trenton Animal Control truck was pulling away from our house. A wire mesh window was in the rear door, and I could see his face through it. Buster, I screamed and raced up the block. Too late, of course. I flew into the house. Why? I yelled. Why?

Just a matter of time till he bit someone and we got sued, said my father. If you weren't so selfish, you'd have known that. I stormed into my room, locked the door and sobbed and sobbed and sobbed. I thought my heart would break into a million pieces. When I couldn't cry any more, my chest kept heaving up and down for a long time. Then I promised myself they'd never make me cry again. And they never did, Mikey. I never cried again for twenty-five years till Carmen's mother died.

That's really why I've never had a dog, Mikey. Not just because I was in the corps. But now I'm ready, pal. I've got a dog again. I made a little prayer the day I decided to keep him. I asked Buster for forgiveness for not somehow saving him. And for giving my love to another dog. And I feel he heard me and said it was OK, Mikey.

Boo hoo, I can hear you crying, Mikey. Alright. Ten four, good buddy. Have a happy Fourth. And keep going to meetings.

SENT: Thursday, September 12, 1991 7:05 AM
To: mailformikey@aol.com
Subject: Power

Mikey, Mikey, Mikey, don't quit the job. I take your word for it that the guy is a putz. Most bosses are. From your description, he's a little guy, a Bantam rooster trying to prove his cojones. Don't threaten his power. It's not real. If it were, he wouldn't be treating his employees like that. Yes him and then do what you want. Chances are he won't even notice. If you finally can't stand it, find another job while you've still got this one. It's always better that way.

Real power never has to prove itself, Mikey. Lemme tell you a story. I visited the island of Bali once. Paradise on earth. I went there on R and R when I was in 'Nam. I hired a guy to drive me across the whole island. The people are as sweet as sugar. Cheery and pleasant, and the women have perfect little boobs. I got to see plenty of them during my tour. Whole Balinese families are bathing in streams along the road as we drive by, and they're all naked. Don't look at them, the driver tells me, that's how we keep our privacy; we're a very modest people so we all agree not to look. I did my best.

We pass a Kentucky Fried Chicken restaurant. The Colonel in paradise. And in front it is a lovely girl about eighteen wearing a sarong on her hips, but nude from the waist up with that perfect little figure. What a beautiful sight, Mikey, walking past a big cardboard cutout of the Colonel.

We come to a temple smack in the middle of the island, run by monkeys. I mean it. Monkeys. There's one Buddhist priest to make sure nobody hurts them, but aside from that, the monkeys have free range of the joint and run it. I have some fruit with me I've taken along to eat on the trip. I get out of the car holding a banana. Right away I'm surrounded by fifteen or twenty monkeys, all staring at the banana. Suddenly, a really big monkey, half again taller than the others, shows up. He comes through the crowd and locks eyes with me. And before I know what's happening, he grabs the banana out of my hand, swallows it in one gulp and throws the peel on the ground. The other monkeys make a dash and fight over it while the big one goes back inside the temple.

Power, Mikey. The big monkey had it. We're all attracted to it. That's why we're fascinated with the Godfather. I met a man of power once. In Mexico. I'm there with Carmen and the shtupper. Carmen is sixteen. We're spending a week at a resort outside Puerto Vallarta. On the beach one day, I strike up a conversation with this guy who's there with his wife and teenage daughter. He's from New Jersey, Mikey, and, as it turns out, is in the liquor transport business. That means he's "connected." Maybe not a "made man," like they say in the movies, but certainly "one of the boys." He tells me how his business runs. In New Jersey, you do not try to transport liquor from warehouse to retail store without having some form of protection. Otherwise, you will find that sand has been poured into the gas tanks of your entire fleet of trucks and the cases of Chivas Regal they were carrying are smashed and their contents dispersed.

The shtupper hits it off with the guy's wife, and Carmen bonds with the daughter. So after a while the guy, Larry, Larry Cohen, a Jew in an Italian business, suggests maybe the shtupper and I would like to join them that evening. They are going into town to a club for dinner and dancing. The girls can stay in the resort because it's one of those self-contained Club Med type setups and completely safe. The girls, of course, are totally thrilled, so we agree to meet the Cohens in the lobby and share a cab into town. When we get to the place, it turns out we're joined by another couple, friends of the Cohens, who are staying at some other place. Cohen hasn't bothered to tell me this. But they turn out to be OK, and we wind up having a good time.

After dinner, Mikey, the other guy, I can't remember his name, says he's going out into the parking lot to smoke a joint, does anyone want to join him? Nobody does, so the guy gets up and leaves. Larry and I go on chewing the rag, and the women do the same. When two couples go out to dinner, the dames always insist on sitting boy, girl, boy, girl. But after a while, the men want to talk guy stuff and the women girl stuff. So everybody has to talk across each other. The women inevitably get up and go to the john together. When they do, the guys switch places, and when the dames come back from the john gabbing away, they don't even notice it.

Meanwhile, in the Mexican club without any of us realizing it, about a quarter of an hour has gone by. Suddenly, Cohen notices his friend has been in the parking lot too long. He says he's going to go out and check on him, and I decide to go along. We walk out the front door of the club and into the parking lot. And what do I see, Mikey, but the guy with a Mexican cop holding him by the arm and a couple more surrounding him. A squad car is there with its lights flashing. Damn, says Larry, and heads over toward his friend. I tag along, curious to see how he's going to handle it. And here's what he does. He reaches into his pocket for his wallet, pulls out a wad of bills and fans them out in front of the head cop. Help yourself, he says, but don't take too much. The cop looks into Larry's eyes and is clearly impressed by what he sees. He takes a couple of bills, looks into Larry's eyes again, and then takes one more. The three of us walk back into the club, and the Mexican cops drive away. I've never forgotten what he said, Mikey. Help yourself, but don't take too much.

I'm glad you're finding good meetings, kid. That sounded hilarious about the stag you were at with the wet drunk trying to take over. What a riot. I remember a wet drunk at a morning meeting one time. It was a five days a week 6:45 a.m. before-work meeting. I used to volunteer to make the coffee and pick up the donuts on Tuesdays and Thursdays so I had to get there even earlier. The speaker finished talking one day, and there was this bum in the back of the room hanging out near me by the coffee and donuts. A real wet drunk, plastered at that hour of the morning, with a butt hanging out of his mouth. He raised his hand to share that the only part of his program that was working was that he was managing to "maintain his anonymity at the level of press, radio and film."

The biggest yuck I ever heard at a meeting, Mikey, was over in the Palisades. In a church. Very Republican. Blue-haired ladies who'd been into the port wine too much. I was the speaker. Well, for some reason two bikers show up. Maybe they needed a meeting and looked in the book, and this one was closest. Anyway, these guys are tattooed and ponytailed and really out of place. Not that they give a damn. They're having the time of their lives. After my talk, it comes time to share, and there's a topic: how low was your bottom? There's low-bottom guys: they're in hospitals, they have no livers, they're hooked up to machines, they're two days away from dying, and they don't think they have a drinking problem. And there's soft-bottom guys: their wives tell them they'll leave them if they don't quit drinking, so they do quit. You know.

So, the blue-haired ladies are sharing their respective bottoms, Mikey. How they left the cucumber sandwiches out in the rain or whatever. Then it comes time for the bikers. I used to snort Sterno, says the one guy. Yeah? Well, I used to pry open my Zippo lighter and drink it, says the other. The poor dames are dying, Mikey. And the guys are getting off on it, trying to outdo each other. So the one guy shares that his only friend was a monkey who used to ride around on his shoulder. Some bum had given it to him to settle a debt.

He's housesitting a friend's trailer in a trailer park at the time. He gets home one night drunker than usual. He gets inside, and the room is spinning. The monkey hops off his shoulder and is perched up on a chest of drawers, looking at him. He manages to get his clothes off and stumble into the shower, trying to sober up. He staggers out of the shower, dripping and naked, and makes it into the bedroom. The monkey is watching him. He falls face down onto the bed and tries to get up, but his arms won't work.

The guy stops talking, and the room is quiet. Finally, one of the kindly blue-haired ladies speaks up. Well, she says, at least you'd hit your bottom. Not quite, says the guy. The monkey tried to fuck me.

Keep the job. Keep going to meetings.

Halloween's coming up. Everything is orange and red. All the flowers have these fall colors. How does God work it out? I've got spiders up the kazoo in my yard. Big, fat orange ones, just like the flowers. Their webs are incredibly beautiful. This morning, there was a huge one all across my front door. I had to stoop down to keep from breaking it. Mind-blowing. Bring Kiera up to see the spiders, Mikey. I can't believe you've never seen my place!

I liked reading what you wrote about your dad. I'm glad you were able to make amends to him even though he's no longer with us. It was a good idea someone had for you to write a letter to him and read it out loud at your meeting. He loved you, Mikey, even if he wasn't the greatest dad in the world. He hurt you, and you hurt him. That's the way it is with fathers and sons so much of the time. He was a good Marine, your dad. Better than he was a father, I'm sure. He saved my life in 'Nam. I've told you about that. He was able to make amends to

71

you before he kicked the bucket. You didn't accept them at the time, but that's OK. Amends don't have to be accepted to work. They just have to be made.

I had to make amends to my dad posthumously, too. And to my mother. My dad was a tough nut, Mikey. Tough? He was impossible. Really cruel sometimes. But I hurt him, too. Life is rough. I don't know what the hell God had in mind. Well, not my business.

The old man stayed on in Trenton, alone in our old house. He kept living there after my mother killed herself. I never told you about that. I guess I never told anyone. It's not something I like to talk about. It was the booze, mainly, I suppose. And my father's affairs. He finally got to the point where he didn't even try to hide them from her. I was eighteen. I'd just graduated High School and enlisted in the corps. I was set to leave for basic training inside of a week. They had one of their usual, horrible fights. Screaming and slamming doors and him smashing her wine bottles in the sink and then walking out the door and heading off to one of his girlfriends' places. By those days, I was just locking myself in my room and playing loud music to try and drown it all out.

Anyway, I left her crying in the kitchen that night and went out to a movie to get away. I suppose I'd hardened my heart to her by then. She wasn't cruel and heartless like my dad, just weak and a drunk. She always loved him no matter what he did to her. I never felt loved by her. Well I suppose I did when I was really little before their marriage turned totally nasty and the booze took hold of her. But whenever she had to make a choice between him and me, it would be him hands down. No matter what he did to her. I never saw him hit her, but his cruelty was worse. Just making her feel like crap all the time so she'd think she couldn't do any better and wouldn't leave him.

When I got back from the flicks that night, there was a squad car with its lights flashing in front of the house and a few neighbors standing around. They wouldn't look me in the eye. The cop came out the door as I was climbing the front stoop and told me what had happened. The neighbors had smelled gas and called them. It's just dumb luck the place didn't blow up. They'd already taken her body away. I walked into the kitchen. There was an empty wine bottle and a glass on the table. She'd spread an old army blanket on the floor in front of the stove and put a pillow there. I guess she wanted to make herself comfortable. She turned on the gas and lay down in front of it. The oven door was still standing open when I got there. And that was that.

I straightened up the kitchen, folded the army blanket and put it away. My pal Frank let me crash on his couch for a few days till it was time to leave for Parris Island. I spoke to my dad once on the phone. He hadn't come home and found out what happened till the next day. He said, "Well, I guess the booze did her in, eh?" I didn't even answer him. There was going to be a little service, but I didn't know who the hell there'd be to go to it. Her parents were dead, and she only had one friend, an old drinking buddy named Ag O'Brien. My father had alienated all his relatives long since and who else was he going to invite? His girlfriends?

I went over to the funeral parlor where they had her laid out and took a look. They'd fixed her up. She'd really been a pretty woman, and now she was again. I couldn't cry, though. Even though I loved her. I guess I'd been stuffing it for so many years to survive in that house, I couldn't really feel anything. I didn't go to the service. I'm sure the corps would have let me show up a day late. But I didn't want to see my father faking some crocodile tears. Probably Ag O'Brien would have been the only one who really missed her.

Anyway, I left and started my new life, such as it was. I wrote him once in a while. He was my father after all, I figured. And I went to see him when I had leave. I didn't want to give up on him completely. I'm not sure why. Some feeling of family, I suppose. Like I said, he stayed on in the house. He pushed away everyone who really cared about him. Except a string of dames who hung around him years on end. Old dames who were apparently into abuse. They competed to be his verbal punching bags. I'd go to visit him, and one of them would always be there. Old schoolteacher types. Not homely, necessarily. Just mousy.

I got to know most of them a little bit over the years, Mikey, because they wrote me letters. My dad used them to say things he wouldn't say. Oh, your father was so proud when you were decorated and your picture was in the paper. He'd never tell me himself, of course. Oh, your father feels so bad when you don't come to see him. Oh, your father is getting frail and shouldn't really be left alone.

I find a message on my machine when I get back from a whitewater rafting trip in Colorado. I've been gone a week, and the call's been waiting for me. It's from the old dame of the day, saying my father's in the hospital. So I phone New Jersey, and it turns out he's been released that afternoon and is on his way home. He's eighty-five by then. He had a fall and couldn't get up from the sidewalk. When they examined him, they found out he was undernourished. He doesn't bother to eat when he's home alone.

He has enough dough. He's perfectly comfortable, as the euphemism goes. But he refuses to take responsibility for himself. He gets the Meals on Wheels they send old people three times a week. He doesn't even open the containers. When one of the dames is there, she sets the food out on the table and makes him sit down and eat it. Then he has a perfectly good appetite. When I go to visit him and take him out to a restaurant, he eats like a bull moose. But when he's alone, forget about it. It's like he'd rather die than admit it's his responsibility to take care of himself.

Anyway, by the time I get the message, he's spent a week and a half in the hospital, and they've fattened him up. He loved the attention from the doctors and nurses, of course. And the old schoolteachers have taken turns coming to see him. They manage to work it out so they're never there at the same time. Sort of a revolving geriatric harem. And of course, he's eaten the clinic out of house and home. He even asks for seconds on Jell-o. But now he's back alone again, and who knows what's going to happen.

After a couple of days, I get a letter from the dame who left the phone message for me. I'm in my eighties now, she writes, and not as strong as I used to be. Why can't he trade her in for two forty-year-olds, Mikey? I try to get over to your father's place as often as I can, she says. He's not well enough to be left alone and doesn't understand his financial situation. So now I've got a real guilt trip laid on me.

Oh God, I tell myself. I guess I've got to fly back east and see what I can do for him. I don't really want to go, Mikey. We've never been close, and I resent having to take care of him. But I call up and tell him I'll come in and spend a few days helping him get his act together. His banking affairs and all. The old guy is delighted and says he'll get all the paperwork ready.

But when I fly there and show up at his house, Mikey, it's a whole different story. The place is a pesthole, first of all. Boxes and boxes of papers and pamphlets and correspondence and God knows what. He's got letters he hasn't answered that were mailed him in the fifties, Mikey. But he won't throw them away. He holds on to everything that comes his way on the grounds he might need it some day. I reach into one of the boxes and come up with a magazine from 1937! Not even an *interesting* magazine. I ask him if there's an article in it he's saving or what, and he says no. So I go to heave it in the trash can. He practically jumps out of his skin. No, gimmie that. There must have been some reason I kept it. And dust is flying all over the place as he goes through the boxes looking for other stuff he must have kept for some reason.

I ask him if he's dug out the papers we talked about on the phone, the bank statements and all. So we can figure out his financial situation. They're around here somewhere, he says, it's alright, I'm in good shape, don't worry about it. And he changes the subject and starts bitching about one of his girlfriends. Wait a minute, I say. I flew in here to help you with this stuff, and you're supposed to have it ready. What about those investments the lawyer made for you? He'd told me that some shyster had gotten him twenty-five grand a few years ago when he was in a bus accident, and the guy had put it into bonds or something for him.

Oh, I don't know where those papers are right now, he says. But it's alright. The lawyer is trustworthy. Well, what's his name, I ask? Whose name? The damn lawyer, dad! Oh hell, I don't remember. It's probably in my phone book somewhere. But of course, we can't find the stupid phone book in the endless boxes of 1937 magazines. So the upshot, Mikey, is there's not a thing I can do for him after flying all the way across the country.

I take him out to lunch at a Chinese joint, and he eats like a warthog, polishing off all his food and half of mine. And that night, we dine Italian. I sleep in my old room, which is now full of his boxes of old crap from the year one, and the next day, I take him out for one last meal, and then I fly home.

I'm so mad at him, I can't see straight, Mikey. I know the day is going to come when I get a call from some hospital, and they say your father is too feeble and disoriented to go home alone. What would you like us to do with him? And what the hell am I going to say, Mikey? I mean, he's too stubborn to let me do anything for him, but at the same time, he acts helpless and wants me to take over.

By the time I get back to L.A., I'm really fuming. I go to my stag meeting and share how I know I'll get that phone call and what the hell am I going to say? Well, I know what I'm going to say, Mikey. It's all rehearsed in my mind. And I give the guys at the meeting my speech.

What would I like you to do with him, doctor? Nothing. I've tried to help him for years, and he won't let me. So, do what you want with him. He owns a house and has enough dough to provide for himself. If you let me know where you put him, I'll come pay him a visit. That's all. I tell the guys that if the time ever comes I lay a load of crap like that on my daughter, Carmen, I hope she'll have the guts to tell me to go stick it.

Well, there's a long pause when I finish sharing. And of course, that annoys the hell out of me. The next guy who shares says he hopes his program has taught him to be more open and loving to his family than I seem to be. I feel like walking out of the damn meeting, Mikey.

But then one of the alcoholics speaks up, a guy named Marshall, who wears a Chicago Bears cap. He says hey pal, you're worrying about something that hasn't happened yet. When the phone rings, God will let you know what to do. The minute he says it, I know he's right, Mikey. I cool down, and some of the other guys start talking about their parents and what they're going to do when they die. The topic turns to death in general, and some guys are saying they're scared of it. It doesn't scare me, Mikey. I faced it down in Korea and 'Nam. There was stuff I went through where dying wasn't the worst option.

I carry one of those stickers in my wallet you put on the back of your license so if they scrape you out of a crash, they know they can take whatever they need. Eyes, kidney, whatever. I used to say that when I died, I was going to leave myself intact to a needy necrophiliac. (Look it up, Mikey.) The sticker's on my Neptune Society card. I joined up a few years ago. I'm in their computer. When I bite the dust, somebody can call, and they'll come get me. They'll nuke me and send me home in a Mason jar. Or they'll sprinkle me at sea if I want. But I figure that's a rotten trick to play on the fish. Anyway, I'd hate to think of myself as litter.

The whole thing about death in this country is so awful, Mikey. It's no fun to die here these days. Once upon a time, it made you the center of attention. Like that grand old painting of General Montcalm breathing his last out there on the field of battle. A blood spot on his fine uniform, but aside from that, he looks swell. And all his officers and men standing there watching him die, respectful and all, their hats in their hands. Nowadays, he'd be hooked up to IVs and carried off by a copter, all noisy, no respect, Mikey. Just because everybody's so scared of death, they won't let poor old Montcalm go in peace. He doesn't look like he minds dying, and neither does anyone else in the painting.

They were used to death in those days, Mikey. Half your kids died before they grew up, maybe more, and you built a box and dug the hole yourself. Wives died, too. Childbirth. Influenza. You see cemeteries in New England with the whole family on the stone. Hezekiah

Farnsworth and his wife, Hepsibah, and his wife, Charity, and his wife, Jezebel. The dames dropped like flies, and the old guy was out on the market again. No wonder there weren't any divorces. Marriage lasted seven or eight years. There wasn't time to get sick of each other.

I used to walk through those old graveyards reading the stones. They put jokes on them, Mikey: "Come and see me sometime." And my favorite: "I told you I was sick."

The Indians had the right idea about death. Those Plains Indians who kept moving. When an old-timer was ready to go, they gave him a chaw of tobacco and found him a nice cave to sit in, looking at the sunset. And off they rode. What a nice way to go. Alone with the Great Spirit. I'm sure those old Indians gave up the ghost real easy when the sun finally set and the tobacco was done. They were right on when it came to dying, Mikey. They knew we're all part of the Great Spirit. And what we call dying is just going home to him. I don't know if any of them believe in reincarnation like the Indian Indians do. It makes sense to me that we come back. I wouldn't mind being a dame next time. Just to see what it's like.

Well, really, what does it matter? Worrying about it is just another way of resisting what's happening now. That's the thought I kept in mind when I got the call and flew back for the old man's funeral. Bye for now, kid. Keep going to meetings.

Do you want to make God laugh? Tell him your plans.

I mean, here I am seven years into the program. By the way, you've got seven months now. Did you realize that? Congratulations. Anyway, here I am feeling great. Got life by the cojones. Got friends to have coffee with. I can walk out of the movie in five minutes without having to negotiate. And I have to go and fall in love. And with a dame who's religious, Mikey. I can't even make a move on her. Well, that's alright. It's been so long I don't even know if the apparatus would work anyway.

I met her in a coffee bar in a Farmers' Market I go to sometimes on San Vicente. A laid-back joint where people sit around nursing their cup and reading the paper. I've seen her there on and off for a couple of years. Sometimes with a guy, sometimes without. I never did anything, figuring she was attached. Anyway, I didn't think I wanted to make a change in my own life. But one morning, something tells me to lay a hello on her. I figure maybe it's God whispering in my ear, and I don't want to make him mad by disobeying.

Her name is Terry. She's forty, I guess. Maybe thirty-nine. Too young for me, but to hell with it. Light brown hair. Green eyes. Fabulous mouth. Great slim figure. Anyway, she's sitting a couple of chairs away from me, holding a grande latte or some damn thing, and I smile at her, and she smiles back. So I follow the instructions from above and say hello. I mean, I'm on automatic pi-lot, I don't even know what I'm doing. I tell her I've seen her here on and off for a while, and she says yeah I've noticed you. And without even deciding to, I pick up my coffee and move over next to her.

It seems to me her face falls a little when I do, I'm not sure. So I say is it OK if I join you for a second? Why for a second, Mikey? A dumb thing to say, but it just comes out of my mouth. I'm excited for some reason. I feel like I'm starting something big in my life, and I'm just say-ing hello to a stranger. I guess she sees the concern on my face, you know, am I being too forward? Such an old-fashioned expression for this day and age. So she smiles and says no, it's fine, I mean yes it's fine. And then she laughs, and the ice breaks and we start talking. And I find everything she has to say so damned interesting, Mikey. So I start telling her all my stuff.

Before we know it, it's time for lunch, and I say why don't we go into the little restaurant there and continue this conversation. She says she's a bit short on cash. I say that's OK, it's on me. She says how about we go in the market, they make great sandwiches, and we could get a couple and come back and eat them out here. I say fine, and we do. I get roast beef on rye. She gets some kind of egg salad on whole wheat.

Our places are taken when we come back, Mikey. It's benches and tables around a big banyan tree. But there's a couple of chairs in the next section over, so we grab those and keep talking while we eat. She's a music teacher in a private school, never been married. I tell her I've been married twice, single for years now, don't date, at least haven't for a long time. I tell her what I do, about my place and the dog and about Carmen and the new baby. Oh jeeze, I just realized I never told you. Sorry. She had a little boy over there in Qatar, and they're making noises about moving back to the States. I'm making a push for here, but they might want to go to Massachusetts to be near his people. I tell her the weather sucks there. The baby is used to hot weather in Arab land, and they should bring him here. It's still a possibility. It depends on Toomajanian's work. We'll see. I keep praying about it.

If they do come here, they could stay in the house next door to me. I think I told you, I own it. I bought it with my mustering-out money. Well, the dough I made when I invested it after I got sober. The joint's rented, but the couple is maybe going to move out soon. It's too much to hope for, but miracles happen, Mikey. And I know I have God's ear on the matter. It's up to him, of course.

I ask her what does she do for fun? She says she's involved in a number of church-related activities. Oy, Mikey. I ask her what kind of a church does she go to, and she says a Lutheran church in Santa Monica. The school she teaches in is connected to it. Martin Luther is the guy who started the whole Reformation. He nailed a bitch list on a door in Germany complaining that priests were selling get-out-of-hell-free cards for big bucks. A book I read said Luther was constipated and the few times he was able to take a fine steaming dump, he felt connected to God. I've always thought that for communion, the Lutherans ought to serve prune juice. I don't mention this suggestion to Terry.

She hands me a little card. It has a picture of Jesus on it and the name and address of her church on the other side. I decide not to tell her about the time I met Jesus. I know I've never told you about that. I've never told anyone. I can't believe I'm telling you now. It was in New York City. I'd been living there for a year after I mustered out. I had an apartment on the thirty-fourth floor of a new building on West Seventy-third Street. Matter of fact, I was the first tenant the joint ever had. It wasn't quite finished yet, but the top floors were done, and I said I didn't mind being alone, so they took my money and let me move in. I was still smarting from my divorce from the shtupper and just wanted to have a clean pad to crash in and drink by myself. I was into white wine in those days—for some reason. Not a good drink for a Marine, but I was out of the corps, just barely with a good conduct discharge, and I didn't feel so macho I had to drink brother Daniels. I suppose I was trying to ease off the booze by shifting down to Chablis.

My apartment was high up and faced south. Nothing but four-story tenements between me and the Empire State Building. And way downtown, I could see the Twin Towers on a clear day. It was summer when I moved in, Mikey. On weekends, all the fancy people went out to the Hamptons. Even back then. I spent most afternoons in Central Park. A short block east, an easy walk. The park was pretty scruffy. They hadn't started keeping the cars out yet, but I still loved it. It was built in Civil War days. Nothing around it but cow pastures. The guy who designed it knew the city would move up and past it. That's why they called it Central Park. Even Saint Pat's down on Fifty-third Street was alone in the middle of a field when it was new. Those city planners were something, Mikey. Maybe my son-in-law will plan a great thing like that some day.

Nights, I hang out in my pad and sit and think. Not a smart thing to do. The thinking part, I mean. I don't feel like going out. I'm depressed and need to be alone. I don't want to make another mistake like I made with the shtupper. I guess I have to be alone as long as it takes to feel OK by myself before I can even think about getting involved with anybody else. Little did I know how long it was going to be.

One night around seven-thirty, I go into the kitchen to look in the icebox. I take out a bottle of Chablis and then put it back. I can't drink, for some reason. There's a pad of eight-by-ten paper on the table. I'd started to write a letter to Carmen that afternoon. I'd gotten as far as Dearest Ca, and the phone had rung, and I'd never gotten back to it. I rip the paper off the pad and fold it in half. I bend the top ends into triangles and then fold them again and crease them down. I'm in my second childhood, Mikey. Making paper airplanes.

I carry the plane to the front window. A Kleenex or something flies by. It's windy out. There's a little footlocker left over from the corps in front of the window. I sit down on it and shoot the plane out the window. It goes this way and that and then heads down to the street. At the last minute, it doesn't crash, but flies back up. I give a cheer, Mikey. The wind starts carrying it east toward Central Park.

The plane is flying along at about a twelfth or thirteenth floor level. It's pretty far away by now, but I can see it. There's still enough light. It comes to the end of the block by the park. Then it sails up and disappears around the corner. I can't believe it. I hang out the window trying to snag another look, but it's gone. I stand up. I'm restless. Stir crazy. But I don't want to go out. I turn on the tube. I have a little seventeen-inch TV in front of my Salvation Army sofa. I channel-surf a while, but there's nothing. I flip the set off and move into the john to take a whiz.

Then I go to the living room again. I flop down on the sofa and stare at the wall. Another night spent just waiting. After a while, I head back to the window and sit down to check out the night. I look up toward the park. Coming around the corner at about a twenty-five-story level, Mikey, is a little speck of white. It flies this way and that, then heads toward me. When it comes closer, I can see it's a paper airplane. I lean out the window. The plane is coming closer. I can't believe it. I launched it a good ten minutes ago. Is it going to come close enough for me to see for sure it really is mine?

It's flying toward me. This is nuts. There are a dozen buildings on my block. There are a hundred-eighty windows on this side of the building (I counted them the next day). And the plane is coming to the one I'm in. It's headed right at me. I'm laughing out loud, Mikey. It arrives. I reach out and grab it and haul it in. It's mine. Dearest Ca is on the wing.

What can it mean, Mikey? What kind of crazy miracle is it? For sure, it's a miracle. Sail a paper airplane out the window, and ten minutes later, it comes back to the same window? But what the hell is the point of a dumb miracle like that?

The point, schmuck, I realize, is miracles do happen and will happen and are happening and you just have to be open to them. Alright, I'm getting to the part about Jesus. It'll take about three seconds. The thing with the plane was a coming attraction. We now skip two weeks ahead. I'm sitting in my apartment on the couch as usual, staring at the wall, killing the night. At quarter past eight, I glance up, and there standing in the hall, Mikey, by the front door, is our Lord and Savior, Jesus Christ. For some reason, it doesn't surprise me. I don't say anything, I don't do anything, I just sit there looking at him. I know it's Jesus. It's real. I know the difference between real and fake. It's as real as anything I've ever experienced in my life. I don't question it for a second.

Jesus just stands there with a little smile on his face. He doesn't say anything either, just stands there radiating peace of mind, peace of soul, peace of whatever for about twenty minutes. Then I glance away, and when I look back, he's gone. And that's it. It was a one-time thing.

Well, it was a miracle, Mikey. But I'm still not sure what to do with it. I believe in miracles, of course. And I know Jesus is alive and well and living in New York. And everywhere else, I suppose. I don't know why he came to see me. I don't know if he's the son of God. I don't know anything. I suppose I'll figure it out in God's good time. I'm not going to tell Terry. I don't want her to think I'm pulling religious rank on her. Or trying to show off or something. I probably shouldn't have told you. I've never told anyone.

And yes, I've seen her again. I asked her out the day I met her. To dinner and a movie. But we never made it to the movie. We just kept gabbing after the meal. We're so easy with each other. I've never felt so relaxed around anyone. I knew it right away, Mikey. I just love her. We've had a few dates. Night before last was the latest. It gets better every time. And I can tell she feels it, too. At least I'm pretty sure she does. Of course, I'm skittish, Mikey. It's been so long. But even if it goes nowhere and turns out to be a heartache, it's worth it. Better to have loved and lost.

Listen to my advice, kid. I'm almost too old to be your father. Keep going to meetings.

I'm looking out the window, watching the sun go down, and it's only three forty-five. God. Time was, I'd have been heading for a bar, I suppose. I was reading one of my science magazines, Mikey, and thinking about how your old man and I used to hang out in the PX together and drink beers and read *Popular Mechanics*. He was funny, your dad, said he never met a popular mechanic. That was his joke every time. We graduated to *Popular Science*, and we'd sit and drink and talk about the new physics, and the more bombed we got, the more we actually thought we understood it. Since I'm sober, I actually do get some of it. Black holes and quarks. And nothing I've ever learned contradicts the idea of God.

Take the subject of time, Mikey: it's always now. It's now now. And now it's now. While you're reading this e-mail, it's now. Finish reading it, and it's still now. Life is an ongoing, continuous succession of moments of now. You can say to yourself, "When tomorrow morning

93

comes, what will I do then?" But the time never comes when you hop out of bed and say, "At last, it's then!" It'll be now tomorrow morning. The same now it is now. It will feel the same because it is the same. The sun rises. The sun sets. It's now. You go to a movie, or you read a book. It's now. We live in the now, Mikey. Always. Time travel is science fiction. Science fact says it's always now. We don't think about it because we're so busy checking out when does the show start or when do we have to get to school. But we're moving along in a river of time. And it's just as real as space and all the stuff that's in it.

It began with the big bang, Mikey. Scientists agree on that these days. They figured it out. They looked in their telescopes and saw how all the stars are running away from each other. Expanding. The expanding universe, they call it. They calculated out how fast they were traveling and then reversed it. Then, they did the math and found out when it began and how big it was in the beginning. Infinitesimal. That was the start of everything. A little pinpoint made of something or other exploded, and a few seconds later, all the ingredients needed to whip up everything in the universe, including you and me and the Milky Way and those Mounds bars you like to eat, just appeared out of it somehow.

Science agrees on this stuff now. You have to accept certain things when the scientists say so. You don't have to go down to the wharf and watch for ship masts to come over the horizon like Columbus did to know the world is round. After a while, you just accept it because the books tell you to. It's the truth we get to operate in for now, Mikey. For convenience. If new books come out later and say the world is flat and carried on the back of a big turtle, you can deal with that later.

The big bang theory means that the universe and everything in it is a certain number of years old. Including time. Before the big bang, there wasn't any time. The explosion happened fifteen billion years ago. That's when they figure it all began. Before the big bang, there was nothing, Mikey. It didn't happen in any context or any space. There wasn't any space. Space came when the big bang happened. The bang was all there was. In those first few seconds, everything that everything else got made of just appeared somehow. And it all started flying around. And galaxies got formed and came apart and got formed again. And one of them was our 'hood, the Milky Way, not a heavy hitter as galaxies go. And in the boondocks of the Milky Way, not in the inner city where the action is, but off in the sticks near the edge, is our little star. And spinning around it as cozy as can be, there's nine little planets. And the third one out is home sweet home, Mikey.

Now, Carl Sagan, who I used to watch late at night on Carson, always said there had to be millions of inhabited planets in our galaxy alone. Which, combined with the trailer-park neighborhood we live in, tends to make us look pretty bush league. But more and more of the guys who stargaze for a living are starting to think that maybe we're the only planet with intelligent life, that our setup may be unique in the cosmos. We're just far enough away from our sun. We have a moon, and it's just the right distance from us. If it was a little bigger, or a little smaller, or a little closer, or a little farther away, we'd either be all ocean or dry as a bone.

It's perfect planning, Mikey. We have just the right amount of water. We keep recycling it. A drunk chugs a six-pack and takes a leak in the weeds. The sun soaks it up, and the next day, it comes back as rain. Maybe you took a shower this morning, Mikey, in the exact same water Moses waded into when he parted the Red Sea.

There are deserts, of course, but they wouldn't be a problem if it weren't for us humans. The world is perfect. The people in North Africa used to move on when the rain stopped and everything dried up. When it started raining again, they came back. They liked it that way, the way circus people like going on the road. But when the dead white guys from Europe stuck political boundaries up, the nomad people were screwed. They had to stay where there wasn't any water and get CARE packages.

These days, everybody's worried about global warming. The ice caps will melt, and New York will be under water! Forty years ago, Rachel Carson wrote a book,

The Sea Around Us. I had a copy of it. She said New York would be flooded in twenty years. It wasn't. In the eighties, *Newsweek* had a story about the coming ice age. Humans are worrywarts, Mikey. It's our nature. We worry about everything. That's why we like scary movies. At least there's not a shark eating us. When I was a kid, I had to see every horror movie the day it came out. I'd play hooky and hop the bus to Newark. Godzilla, Rodan, The 50 Foot Woman. In the fifties, when the Russians were going to nuke us, there were all these movies about giant bugs. We were scared of fallout and mutations. That was Einstein's little present to us.

He was the one who told President Roosevelt to build the bomb. Einstein changed everything. He had all these wild ideas, and they turned out to be true. There isn't any matter, Mikey. Nothing is solid. It's all just energy that looks and feels real. You're not really there, in a physical sense. I'm not really here. We're probably all just thoughts in the mind of God. And that's not as far out as it seems, Mikey. The new quantum physics is finding out incredible stuff. The steel in the Chrysler Building and the Mounds bar that's probably in your pocket are made of atoms that are 99 point 999999999 percent empty. That's a lot of nines, Mikey. There's nothing there but energy. And they're starting to find out the energy is made up of information. We're literally living in the information age. We are the information age. The human body is so complex and smart. I don't mean brain smart. I mean every little atom in you and me has a job to do and knows how to do it. Every gene. There's a wisdom in us, and in caterpillars and squirrels, that seems to have been put there by God.

My tenant's wife had a baby. I told you about them. They're just nice, laid-back folks. They take good care of the place and don't call me every time the toilet backs up. So I rent it to them cheap. It's the other house on my property. He mows the grass and waters the flowers, too. It's part of the deal. Anyway, I go to visit her at Saint John's, and while I'm there, the nurse in charge of teaching new mothers about breast-feeding comes in. She says an amazing thing, Mikey. When a mother kisses her newborn baby, she inhales its breath. And the baby's breath contains all the information about what the baby needs. So the mother's milk adapts to fill the baby's needs. Every mother's milk is a little bit different, Mikey. They've done tests at Saint John's. That's what I mean about the wisdom that's in us. Not in our brains. Not information we learn growing up. But wisdom that's in every cell of our body.

And who put it there, Mikey? Who drew up the plans for the whole gorgeous world we live in and the light show we call the cosmos? The intellectual elite ain't so intellectual. They say they rely on science, but they don't ask the hard questions scientists are supposed to ask, like what came before the big bang? Forget faith, Mikey. Forget religion. Science pretty much agrees that everything including time started with the big bang. Well, who lit the fuse? Whoever or whatever lit the fuse was eternal. Was there before time and space. Was all wise and powerful. That sounds like a definition of You-Know-Who to me. Call it what you want, but don't pretend it isn't there and ignore it like the brainy types do. Ask the hard questions, and don't settle for not getting an answer. There are scientists at work on it, Mikey, working in quantum physics and molecular biology, and they're going to come up with answers.

Don't get me wrong. It's not Creationism. That's a lot of silly fake science. Creationism says dinosaur fossils don't mean anything and the planet's only six thousand years old. What I'm talking about is real subatomic and molecular science. In another twenty or thirty years, the guys working in it are going to prove their case. And then all hell is going to break loose, like it did with Einstein.

Look. For centuries people believed in God because they had no choice. There wasn't any science to speak of, no other explanation for why the sun popped up every day and went to bed at night. Then, Copernicus and Newton started coming up with explanations that didn't need God. And Darwin was frosting on the cake. Yippee, we weren't created, we evolved! But Darwin never said that. He wrote about turtles and birds. Darwin was a believer.

The real scientists working on this stuff say evolution's only part of what happened. But the evolution types are stubborn. One time, a bunch of them had a convention in Chicago. They flew in some big math geniuses and asked them to figure out how many billion years it would have taken for the first little amoebas or whatever to evolve into human beings. The professors went in the other room with their paper and pencils and came back with the answer. They said there wasn't enough time, so it couldn't have happened that way. The evolutionists said well, it did happen that way, so your math must be wrong. You think I'm stubborn.

It's complicated, Mikey, but it's simple, too. If an all-knowing, all-loving, all-powerful creator set up the whole thing, it's totally simple. It's only complicated to figure out if we insist it all happened by accident. God, I wish your dad was still here. I'd love to get into all of this with him. There are billions of galaxies with billions of stars in them. And now it turns out our little planet may be the only one with intelligent life. How can we be the only one in the whole universe? Because nature is profligate. Wasteful. It likes to be. Look. The average guy in America has something like two-and-a-half kids. Right? (That means somebody has four because I only got one.) But that guy ejaculates thousands of times in his life, and every time he does, he shoots out millions of sperms. Billions in his lifetime. And every one of them contains all the information needed to reproduce the guy. Talk about waste! Nature doesn't care. Billions of sperms for two-and-a-half kids. Billions of stars for one little planet.

The numbers are mind boggling, Mikey. Do you know that 10 percent of the gross weight of every living thing on earth is ants? Ants, Mikey! Do you know that the distance between the stars is so huge that if you shrank the size of a star to a pinpoint, only three of them would fit inside the Grand Central Station. There are miracles all over. The new physics types say everything has awareness in it. A turnip has a little. A person has a lot. Matter is energy, and energy is information. Wisdom. We're made up of God's wisdom.

Hard to understand? I don't even try, Mikey. I just invite it in. I let it marinate a while and see what I come up with. God, I miss your dad. Glad things are good with Kiera. I asked Terry over here one afternoon. I watched her looking around, sizing up the joint the way women do, figuring out if it could be a nest. I think she liked the house. Old twenties pseudo-Craftsman. All my stuff is so masculine, though. Leather furniture, naval battle lithographs on the wall. She hated the big new windows I just put in. White coated aluminum. She didn't say anything, of course, but it was radiating off her.

She loved the yard. There aren't many yards this big in Santa Monica. Huge ficus trees and a big old Jacaranda in the corner. Not in bloom this time of year, but she knows how amazing it will be in the spring. She glanced at the rental house. I could see her mind working. How much dough does this guy have? Christian or not, women are always sizing up guys as potential providers. It's instinctual.

I want the woman in my life, Mikey. I'm determind to get her in here. Screw the new aluminum windows; I'll rip them out! I'm living in my own soap opera: The Old and the Horny. Keep e-mailing me, kid. Keep going to meetings.

SENT: Tuesday, May 12, 1992 11:04 PM
To: mailformikey@aol.com
Subject: Trouble

It was so good to see you, Mikey. And I'm so proud of you. Clean and sober a full year. And I'm the one who got to give you the cake. When you blew out the candle and thanked your Higher Power, I almost burst. And keeping you clean and sober isn't the only thing he's doing. Don't tell me it's a coincidence you met a girl like Kiera when you got your act together. It was great to see her sitting there next to you. An adorable little thing, no bigger than the palm of your hand. But (as the old joke goes) better.

That was a lively meeting, Mikey. I liked it. Good energy. And I loved getting to see where you lived. A great little pad. San Diego at its best. Kiera seems pretty much to have moved in. I noticed the two toothbrushes in the glass in the john.

I wanted to invite Terry to take the train down with me, but, well, something came up. We've been six months together, and as I've told you, I'm nuts about her. So on

Thursday, I made a decision. I went to the May Company and bought a ring. Hold your congrats, Mikey. There's more to the story.

I took her out tonight and wined and dined her. Well, iced tea-ed and dined myself. And while we're into the chocolate soufflé I ordered for dessert, I put the little box with the ring in it on the table in front of her and tell her it's for her. You can keep it or let me have it back or throw it away, I tell her. I know I'm too old for you, I say, but I come from good stock, at least agewise: my people live a long time. Anyway, a gorgeous dame like you should worry? The new guy will take you to the funeral.

She opens the box and takes the ring out. It's beautiful, she says, and gives me a kiss on the cheek. The waitress walks by just then and says congratulations. Terry looks at the ring a minute. Then she sticks it back in the box. She takes my hand and says it's awful quick. She says she's forty years old and never been married, and there must be reasons for that. She says she's probably put up walls around herself. I tell her I've got ladders.

She reminds me that I am a lot older than she is. I feel like I should start singing "The September Song" (look it up). I'm ready for all her arguments, Mikey. I tell her most marriages end up in divorce these days. People get seven, maybe ten good years and then everything falls apart. So she can have twenty-five or thirty good ones with me and still wind up young enough to be the hot young widow at the old folks home. Laughs I can get out of her, Mikey. Yes isn't so easy.

There's another thing, she says, and she brings up the "J" word. Jesus. She tells me she knows I met him and all. Yes, I finally told her that a few dates ago. She says she's sure I love God in some generic way, but she doesn't see how she could ever marry a man who isn't a real Christian, who doesn't accept Jesus as the only begotten son of God. Her actual words, Mikey. Heavy. Wall number one.

I take a deep breath and start my pitch. I tell her she's never going to find a man who loves God more than I do. I say I'm sure her church is full of people who say Jesus is the only way to salvation and then cheat on their taxes and their wives. The minute the words are out of my mouth, I know I've screwed up. Her face gets really dark. You don't know that she says. I've asked you to come to church with me and you never have.

I'm starting to get hot under the collar now too, Mikey. I tell her I love God in my way, why can't she love him in hers? I say I don't know if Jesus is his son. How can that be? Did God come down one night when Joseph was out building a wheelbarrow and dip the wick in his wife? Oh jeeze, Mikey, that does it. My temper, my well-known fast, sharp, stupid tongue.

That's really not nice, she says. She suggests I take her home so we can both cool down and think things over.

She tells me I have no idea how important her Christianity is to her. It's her whole life, she says. It would be more important to her than her marriage if she did say yes to me. Like a schmuck, I ask what about the ring? The Dark One is putting inappropriate words in my mouth. Tears come into her eyes. She says maybe I should hold on to it for now. At least she says for now, Mikey. She says she understands what I'm asking, and she's really touched, but she needs some time. The *Newsweek* story about the ice age comes in my mind. I ask for the check, and we both just sit there at the table. The waitress gives us a funny look. I leave her a nice tip, and we get out. When we're on the sidewalk in front of the restaurant, I take hold of her and began what feeble damage control I can muster up.

I'm so sorry, Terry, I say. I was out of line in there. I tell her I have a bad habit. I say nasty things sometimes and then regret them two seconds later. I tell her I really do love God, and I guess I love Jesus, too. And I guess he must love me, I say, or he wouldn't have paid me that visit. I'm really warming to the subject again, Mikey. And while my mouth is moving, as it usually is, Old Mephisto squirts some three-in-one oil in it. I say the whole business of God sacrificing his only son to save us from our sins is iffy to me.

In the Old Testament, I tell her, Abraham gets the word he has to sacrifice his kid to prove he loves the Boss. In the New Testament, it's God proving his love, so he has to sacrifice *his* kid. No one knows for sure, I say, if Jesus was born in a manger and visited by wise men.

She interrupts me, Mikey. I know for sure, she says. The bible says so. That's all I need. I have faith. That's what you don't understand. You're so much smarter than I am, and you've figured everything out. But it's not the same as coming to it by faith. Faith, she says, is what gives her strength, not knowledge or intuition or facts. Or even a personal visit from Christ. You told me yourself that didn't change you, she says. She stops talking and looks at me a while. Then she puts her head on my shoulder. She says she loves me, but she's not sure love is enough. She thinks we need to be going in the same direction, and she's not sure we are. Oh God, Mikey.

I feel really shook up. The evening has not gone as planned. I decide the best thing I can do is take her home. And that's what I do. We don't say another word on the way back to her place or even when we get to her door. Not even goodnight. I hold her for a while and then let her go. It's been three days. I did call once, when I knew she'd be at work, and left a message saying I loved her. I don't know what to do, Mikey. It seems like a rock and a hard place. I can't make myself believe something I don't believe, and she can't make herself unbelieve it. But I love the woman, and she says she loves me. She does. I know she does. Maybe I'll go to church with her if she'll still have me. I dread it. Perhaps I'll take a crack at the bible.

Well, Mikey, I'm glad one of us is getting some action. Give Kiera one for me. I'll just go to bed and curl up with Leviticus.

Keep going to meetings.

SENT: Saturday, May 16, 1992 7:31 PM
To: mailformikey@aol.com
Subject: A Glimmer of Hope

The dog's name is Ralph, Mikey. That's where I buy his Alpo. At Ralphs. I didn't want to name the poor mutt Alpo, so I named him Ralph. It's a good name for a dog. Nothing fancy, just a good solid name. Here Ralph. It sounds good. There's a beach not far from my place where people get together at 6 a.m. There's no dogs allowed on Santa Monica beaches. They enforce it from seven on, but at six in the morning, the cops wink at it, and sometimes there's thirty, maybe forty dogs racing on the sand, having the time of their lives, catching Frisbees and wrestling on the beach. The cops know the owners will pick up after them and go home by seven, so they don't say anything. It's an hour of pooch paradise just about every day. I've taken him twice, Mikey, and the third time was this morning. He's got a dog collar now, and I found a red bandana in a thrift shop and tied it on him. It's what the well-dressed pooch will wear.

Today is the fourth day Terry and I haven't spoken. I guess she figures the ball is in my court, and really, she's right. But I just haven't known what to say except I love you, and I've already said that. Well, as luck would have it, Ralph is playing with this one dog, another part-time shepherd, birds of a feather, Mikey. And I strike up a conversation with the guy who owns him. Nice-looking guy in his early thirties. We chat for a while. The dogs, the weather, this and that. Then I ask him what does he do? He's a youth counselor at a church. What church, I ask? I can't believe it. He names the church Terry goes to and teaches at. Believe in coincidence, Mikey. You know how I feel.

So I ask him does he know Terry? Know her, he says, he used to go out with her. My face falls, and the guy sees it. Oh my gosh, he says you must be . . . He's laughing. I say how do you know about me? He says Terry and I are friends, and she keeps me up to date on her life. And if you are the guy, she's really crazy about you. I guess I turned red, Mikey, and he laughs some more, explaining that when they used to go out, he meant as friends. I'd have liked a bit more, the guy said, but she said I was too young. And since we were both Christian, it was either marriage or friendship. So, friends is what we are. Oh my gosh, he says again. What a coincidence we should run into each other like this.

Notice the oh my gosh, Mikey. Really Christian. Well, it seems he hasn't seen her in a week. School's out for the summer, and he was away the Sunday before running a youth group in the mountains. So how are you two doing, he asks? And, figuring God has sent Ralph to me so I'd take him to run on the beach and meet this guy, I tell him, Mikey. I open my mouth and blah, blah, blah, tell him everything. More than he wants to know, probably. But I figure he's a preacher-in-training and it's good for him to hear people's stuff. I leave out the part about being a personal friend of Christ the Lord. Never know how a Christian is going to take that. I tell him about us and then shut up and wait for him to give me some good preacherly advice.

It's seven now, and the crowd is breaking up, people going home with their dogs. Neither of our animals has crapped in the sand so we're free to go, too. He says there's a little place a few blocks up the beach where we can tie the dogs up and sit and have coffee. I say let's go, and we stick the leashes on our guys and start up the walkway. When we get to the place, it's a little joint I've seen for years, but never tried. Burgers all afternoon, coffee and bagels in the a.m. The dogs have bonded like boys and are happy to be tied up together. I insist on paying for the java, and we sit down at one of the rickety tables and look out at the Pacific.

It's the biggest thing on earth, Mikey, the Pacific. All the continents in the world could be plunked down in it, and there'd still be room left over. They think the moon came out of it: scientists, whatever they're called, the guys who study origins of things. Planets get ripped out of suns, and moons get ripped out of planets. I'm not talking a week ago Thursday, Mikey. This is before anything, when there were big balls of fire, and everything was being formed. There was one big continent in the earliest days. Then there came a super quake, and Europe and Africa split up and moved away from North and South America. You can still see how they'd fit together if you look on the map. The water that rushed in became the Atlantic. They have a name for that old continent. I used to know it. And on the other side, when the moon got ripped out, the hole it left became the Pacific Ocean. That's what they say, and who am I to say no?

So the guy and me, his name is Barry, look out at the Pacific, and he begins to talk. I was raised Catholic, he says. My uncle was a Jesuit priest. Uncle Father Jim. That's what he calls the guy, Mikey, Uncle Father Jim. I guess he was his mother's older brother, the priest, and he was full of stories. When Barry was a kid, he'd talk to him about the Jesuits. They're educators, intellectuals, but they deal with faith. And Barry says their brains tend to screw with their faith. That wasn't the expression he used, Mikey. In the lobby of the Jesuit headquarters in Rome, he says there's a statue of Saint Ignatius Loyola, the founder, and on the base, it says Go Forth and Set the World Ablaze. But on the wall next to it is a fire extinguisher. That's the split in the Jesuit Fathers. They're too smart to be in the business they're in.

This guy Barry believes faith has to do with acceptance and obedience, and nothing else. Sounds pretty mackerel snapper to me. That's what we called Catholics when I was a kid. On account of fish on Friday, I guess. He says what God requires of us is to obey him. We don't have to understand him. We shouldn't even try. If we obey him, we get out of conflict with our true natures, and we're happy. It's as simple as that, Mikey. That's what the guy says. He says Jesuits like his uncle make it way too complicated. Then he looks at me and says he figures from the few times Terry has talked about me, that maybe that's what I do, too.

God, Mikey. Here's a guy I meet half an hour ago, and he already knows more about me than I do. I'm pretty sore at that point, and I guess it shows. I don't say anything, and the both of us just sit there a while looking out at the big hole where the moon used to live. We finish our coffee, and Barry says lemme get us a refill. I nod okay, and he takes the cup out of my hand and goes to the counter. He's up there a while. There's a line by then. I watch him ask for two paper bowls of water and carry them over to the boys. Then he picks up our coffees and brings them back to where I'm sitting.

I ask him why he's not a Catholic anymore. He says he got sick of the saints and the novenas and the catechisms and all the rest of it. He tells me Martin Luther was a good Catholic, and he couldn't take it either. I ask if he ever misses any of it, and he says yes, he misses going to confession. He laughs and says, of course, he doesn't miss having to tell the Father about "touching myself in an impure manner," but he misses the relief he felt after all the Our Fathers and Hail Marys he had to do.

But the main reason he left, he says, was because of his uncle. He was so brilliant and tortured. So torn apart by his need to understand and to have faith. I say since science is going to prove pretty soon that God exists, why would his uncle have to feel conflicted? He thinks a minute, Mikey, and then he says faith and obedience are what provide peace of mind. Not understanding. He says you can't have both at the same time. And his uncle couldn't stop trying. He couldn't stop, and he couldn't stop, and he finally drank himself to death over it.

What he says hits me like a ton of bricks, Mikey. I don't say anything for a while and neither does Barry. We sit there watching the dogs play. Barry's dog is lying on his back, and Ralph is pretending to rip his throat out, but gently and playfully, and they both love it. Finally, I stand up and shake his hand and thank him. He gives me a card and says we should stay in touch.

I walk home, pulling Ralph a little faster than he wants me to. When we get to the house, I sit down at the little table where my phone lives and dial her number. It rings five times or six times, Mikey. My heart's beginning to sink. Finally she picks up. It's me, I say. She says hi. I say if it's OK, I'd like to come to church with you tomorrow. There's a pause. I can feel her smiling over the phone. I go to the eleven o'clock service, she says. It's a fifteen-minute walk from my apartment. I'll pick you up at ten, I tell her. We can walk slow. She laughs.

I hang up the phone, feel good for the first time all week, and get on the magic machine to you. It feels so good to be able to share this stuff. That's what friends are for, I guess. E-mail me, kiddo. I haven't heard from you in a couple days. Adios.

And keep going to meetings.

Mikey, it's good news. I get a call from Brunei or Arab Emirates or wherever the hell Toomajanian has taken my daughter, and they're coming back. Not just back, but here, Mikey, to L.A. And they want to know can they rent the house next door. The two of them and little Aram. That's my grandson. It's an Armenian name. Maybe Vascan's father or something. Who cares. He's almost one now, and boy, am I dying to see him! They're coming here and want to live in my other house. Can you believe it? I've hardly dared pray about it. But I have. Every day.

It can happen because the couple that was living there moved out and left town in April. I've been letting Marshall with the Chicago Bears cap stay there. I charge him next to nothing with the understanding he'll vacate the joint on a few weeks' notice. It will probably take them six months to wind things up over there. They should be here by Christmas. I'll get the

117

place painted up spick-and-span. I'll buy a swing set and a slide and stick it in the yard, and it will be ready when they get here. I don't know how long they'll stay. Maybe forever, who knows? It depends on Toomajanian's job. But they're optimistic. Some big architectural firm has hired him sight unseen because of his reputation and his work. It's almost too good, Mikey. I keep waiting for the other shoe to drop. I know, I know. It's in God's hands.

Alright. To Terry. Here's what happened. I picked her up at her place Sunday morning. I've brushed my teeth, gargled with Scope, and I've got everything on me but a clean white handkerchief and Sen-Sen. I'm nervous as a cat because I'm going to church, Mikey. Church, that I've sworn I'd never be caught dead in.

When I ring the bell and she comes to the door, my heart practically jumps out of my mouth. I haven't seen her for a week, and I've forgotten how beautiful she is. I hug her, and I can feel the gratitude coming off her. I'm giving her what she wants. At this point, I'm ready to start warbling "The Old Rugged Cross" or any damn thing she asks for.

We leave her place and start walking real slow, like I suggested. I'm thrilled to be with her, but I'm a wreck because of where we're headed. I know it's crazy, Mikey, but I don't want anyone to see me walking into a church. Christian. Yuck! Dressed up, hair combed, and holier than thou.

When I was a kid, my father used to tell a joke over and over. An apple and a dog turd are floating down the river. They float for three days, and finally the dog turd says we've been floating a long time, haven't we! And the apple says where the hell do you get that *we* stuff? I know it's not funny. It's a sour joke, but that was him.

The old man used to say don't make friends with the neighbors, they'll only want something from you. Whether I like it or not, I suppose I inherited some of that suspicious nature from him. I've never had a lot of friends, Mikey. I've loved women, and married some, but I've never had many real friends. Well, there was your dad, and now there's you, Mikey.

Terry and I keep walking, and at the end of every block or so, we stop and hug each other. Well, to be honest, I stop and hug her. I'm putting off the inevitable, and I know she knows it because she starts looking at me funny. Finally she says what's going on with you?

Alright, I say, I'm nervous. I feel like I'm going to meet your folks, and I don't know if they're going to like me or not. It isn't really true, Mikey. What I'm really thinking is what if I don't like them? I don't know why I'm driving myself nuts over it. I've hardly set foot in a church or known any church people in my life. Not that ignorance has ever kept me from having an opinion.

We finally get there. It's a sweet little church on a street loaded with trees. The school is in the back, the bell is clanging away in the steeple, and the whole thing is Norman Rockwell's America. People start waving and nodding at her, and one of the first guys to come up and say hello is Barry from the beach. For some reason, I feel a little jealous when he puts his arm around her. I know they never did anything. He told me that, and I believe him. I guess it's because they go to church together and she tells him all her stuff, and sometimes intimacy with no sex can get pretty deep. I suppose, to be really honest, I'm just scared. One time in Da Nang, I had to stick a bayonet in some poor bastard. I wasn't scared then. Now I'm scared.

Barry attaches himself to us, which kind of annoys me, and we walk into the church. The decor is lovely and simple. White stucco walls and thick dark-wood beams on the ceiling. The stained-glass windows show Jesus doing this and that: healing the poor, getting born, doing the loaves and fishes trick. Quite tasteful, though. The biggest window has the Ten Commandments on two tablets. Commandments one through three are on the first tablet, and the other seven are crowded onto tablet number two. Why, I wonder?

There's a big wooden cross behind the altar, and over to the side, a little band is setting up. Piano, drums, two horns and a couple of guitars. There are four or five mikes standing there, which I assume will be for singers. Terry points out a big pipe organ in the balcony at the back of the church. It gets played in the 8 a.m. service, she says, which is the more traditional one. Mostly older Lutherans who don't want their religion interfered with or improved on. The eleven o'clock service is called contemporary. The parishioners are starting to drift in. Young couples, some old ladies, of course. Teenagers, which surprises me, and quite a few young kids. Maybe that's on account of the church school Terry teaches at. The kids come over and give her hugs and hi's. They seem to love her.

I play piano with the band, you know, she says to me. I hadn't known. I'll leave you here with Barry and see you when the service is over. She takes off and joins the other musicians. Barry starts making small talk with me. We sit in a pew about halfway up to the altar. I make sure I can see the piano from there. In a few minutes, I forget whatever negative thoughts I had about him and remember how friendly he was when I met him at the beach.

I know you said you don't go to church much, he says. I say they baptized me when I was a baby, and I haven't been back since. I tell him that where I grew up in New Jersey, the kids were all Catholic: Italian or Irish. They came from big families. Lots of brothers and sisters. I was an only kid. My parents tried it once and didn't much like it, I guess. I missed having brothers and sisters a lot. So, I'd go hang out at other kids' houses. I liked to hear the arguments around the dinner table. They were different from the arguments around our table. Big families screaming at each other is fun. This is all stuff I've probably told you, Mikey.

On Ash Wednesdays, I tell the guy, I'd go down to the coalbin in our basement, rub some coal dust on my finger and stick a mark on my forehead so I'd look like I'd been to Mass. I wanted to fit in, wanted to be one of the boys. But I didn't like church and neither did my parents. I don't know why they bothered to baptize me in the first place since they never went to church themselves. I guess it was just the thing to do. The guy seems interested, Mikey. Or maybe it's just Christian politeness.

On Sunday mornings, I tell him, my father would sit up in bed. He'd read the paper and curse at the news. Whatever was happening, he'd curse at it. My mother would bring him breakfast on a tray, and he'd dip the toast in his eggs, curse at the news and yell at her to bring him more coffee and make it snappy. That was how we worshipped the Lord in our house on Sundays.

The preacher stands up in front of the altar and starts things off by welcoming everybody. Barry whispers to me that his name is Pastor Ken, he's the greatest, you're going to love him. I've been so busy gabbing, I haven't noticed that Terry is sitting at the piano and the rest of the band is in place. Four singers are standing at the mikes, ready to go into their act. The preacher is a pleasant-looking guy of forty-five or so with thinning hair and a cheery smile.

At this point, Mikey, everyone hops up and begins running around shaking hands and hugging each other. Christian hugs. Ugh. Barry introduces me to this one and that one. They all give me big loving smiles and hearty handshakes, and here and there, a Christian hug. One fabulous-looking dame of thirty or so gives me a Christian hug that for some reason I don't mind at all. Then the band strikes up the first number, and Barry excuses himself. He gets up and leaves. I look over to see how Terry is doing. Well, it turns out she's wailing. The selection is a Black gospel number. Totally unexpected for a Lutheran church. And Terry is banging on the keys like an African-American Baptist in Alabama. The horns and guitars are wailing too, and now the singers chime in. The place is rocking. What would Martin Luther say? Well, maybe he'd love it. He was a muckraker after all.

The congregation is clapping and stomping like they don't know they're white. What a nice surprise, Mikey. The next number is more laid back, and then the last one is my favorite. "I'm coming back to the heart of worship, and it's all about you, it's all about you, Jesus. I'm sorry Lord for the thing I've made it, when it's all about you, It's all about you, Jesus."

Now comes a children's message and, to my surprise, out pops Barry. He asks all the young kids to come up and sit on the steps in front of the altar. They're adorable. A dozen or so of them ages three to maybe eleven.

Barry does some shtick with a prop fireman's hat that makes them laugh. Then he ends up with a prayer, which the kids repeat after him, sitting there with their hands clasped together, looking just as cute as can be. When the prayer is over, Barry announces there'll be Sunday school in the back, and they all go racing down the aisle about seventy miles an hour. So adorable, Mikey. If I'd had something like that when I was their age, maybe I wouldn't hate church so much. In fact, maybe I wouldn't be as much of a curmudgeon as I am in general.

Now it's time for the main course, and Pastor Ken takes over. I look over in the direction of the piano and make contact with Terry. I suppose she's been keeping an eye on me to see how I'm reacting. She gives me a big smile, and it warms my heart to see her so happy. The pastor's sermon is on some subject or other. To tell the truth, I don't remember, Mikey, because once I make eye contact with Terry, I can't really think of anything else. I know the guy mentions Jesus quite a bit. I know he gets quite a few laughs, and when he does, I laugh along with the crowd, even though I don't really hear the joke. I suppose he's quite moving because I feel quite moved. Moved at being in church and finding I don't hate it. Moved at how lucky I am to be alive, Mikey. Like Marshall used to say, another day above ground. The warm California sun is shining through the stained-glass windows with Jesus's picture on them. My woman is getting ready to tickle the ivories for the collection plate special. The kids are back in children's church, and all's right with the world.

When the service is over, people line up to shake the parson's hand. I take the opportunity to go up and thank the band for their music. I'm a friend of Terry's, I introduce myself. From the way they look at me, I have a hunch they know exactly who I am. It's obvious the woman I hope to make my own is very well liked in these parts. I offer congratulations all around and then move in the direction of the piano, where Terry is gathering up sheet music and folding it into the piano bench.

You blew me away, I tell her. You play like an angel. She looks pleased. Let me introduce you to Pastor Ken, she says, and steers me to the back of the church. By now, the line is dwindling down. He's standing in the side doorway. I look past him, and I can see the kids who were on the steps for the children's service racing around in the school playground. When the lady in front of us leaves, Terry introduces me to her pastor. He takes my hand and shakes it and holds on to it. He looks me in the eye. He takes his time. He smiles. He says I'd like to buy you a beer. He doesn't drink, says Terry. A cup of coffee, he says, without missing a beat.

My head is spinning, Mikey. OK, I say. When? he says. I start to laugh. You guys work fast around here. Terry is one of our prized possessions, he says. We don't let go of her easily. He's still holding on to my hand. Alright, I say. Tomorrow afternoon at four. Tomorrow is my day off, but for you I'll make an exception, he says. There's a joint on Wilshire with coffee for you and a beer for me. He writes out the address.

I go reeling out of that church, Mikey, feeling like I've been through some kind of an initiation ritual. Terry holds on to my arm, and we walk over to Fourth Street and have brunch at the English Pub. Then, it's home for me and writing to you. I'll let you know what happens with the pastor. Hang in there, lad. Keep going to meetings.

SENT: Monday, May 18, 1992 7:41 PM
To: mailformikey@aol.com
Subject: The broken drum

My date with Torquemada the Inquisitor: I show up early, about ten to four, so I can sit in the Honda and collect my thoughts. The joint is something out of a time machine. It's called "The Broken Drum: You Can't Beat It." Get it? Har har. I'm in the parking lot in the back and figure I'll see him when he drives in.

By five past, he hasn't shown up yet, and I start to think maybe he got here even earlier than I did and he's inside already. So I lock the car, as if anybody would steal that heap. I push open the door to the restaurant. It's dark in there. Probably a place for serious roast beef eaters who like to start with a Manhattan or two. He's not there. Neither is anybody else, so I pull up a stool and sit down at the bar to wait. The place is hilarious: leather banquettes, flocked red wallpaper, the whole nine yards.

Another ten minutes go by, and I'm starting to think I dreamed the whole thing. Maybe I never met the guy, maybe I never met Terry, maybe I'm not even me, maybe I'm a character in somebody else's dream. Do you re-

127

member conversations like that when you were a kid, Mikey? Twelve or thirteen? What's the nature of reality? Is there a God? Are we all just living in his dream and when he wakes up, will we cease to exist?

I had a friend back then. A kid who loved to talk. Carl was his name. Fourteen years old and he just loved to buttonhole people and bend their ears. He'd talk to anyone. He knew a lot, he was interesting, Mikey, but once he had your ear, he'd never leave any white space so you could say you had to go. His mother laughed once and told me Carl was home alone one day. She'd been gone for an hour or so grocery shopping and when she got back to the house, she said, she found Jehovah's Witnesses trying to get *out*.

Finally, Pastor Ken comes hustling in. Sorry, sorry. He had an emergency. One of his old parishioners fell down and broke her hip, and he had to go see her in the hospital. I tell him it sounds like a pastor's work is never done. Never, he says, that's why I'm going to have a beer. He looks around trying to find someone to wait on us. I tell him if he wasn't a pastor, we could just go behind the bar and help ourselves. He laughs, Mikey, really loud with a weird kind of bray. Then he goes over to the kitchen door and yells whadaya have to do to get some service around here?

The bartender comes running out, laughing. Hey, preacher man, he says, you're early today. Pastor Ken asks him to get a Bud for him and could he hustle up a cup of coffee "for my wimpy friend here?" Preacher humor, Mikey. The bartender goes back into the kitchen and gets my coffee and then goes behind the bar and pulls a pint for the pastor. Then he goes in the kitchen again and leaves us on our own. The pastor says why don't we move over and sit at one of the booths. Yeah, I say, it's more like a confessional. Again that braying laugh, Mikey. It's infectious.

When we're in the booth, he asks me how I met Terry. I tell him I picked her up at a Farmers' Market. I'd seen her there on and off for a while, but one morning, God had whispered in my ear to go for it. He laughs again and says you seem to have a direct line to the Maker. I tell him I think everybody does, they just don't pay their phone bills. Haw haw, he goes. That bray again. I'm getting big laughs from this guy. So you invited her out and started seeing each other? That's the nutshell version, I say. He asks about my twelve-step program. I say that's how I found God, Pastor. He says please call him Ken. I tell him how the twelve steps are about miracles. Enough miracles in your life and your resistance goes away.

He asks me why I have a problem with Jesus. I figure Terry must have been filling him in on me. I tell him the problem I have is with dogma. This is getting heavy, Mikey. Jesus gets crucified, I say, then comes back to life and goes bodily up to heaven? Heaven was up because the world was flat back then. Now the world is round, so what does up mean? Blah blah blah. The same stuff I've been laying on you for months.

I say I know I'm prejudiced. I've always had a thing against the church. I figure I might as well admit it, Mikey. Yesterday, I found out maybe I was wrong, I tell him. But having to accept a lot of stuff in the bible that frankly sounds nonsensical puts me off. At this point I don't know if he's going to smack me, Mikey. But he just has that preacher smile on his face. I'm sure he's used to this stuff.

You have no problem with God, he says? I tell him I see proof of God every day. And not just in the miracles of the program. Why would spiders spin beautiful webs, I say, when ugly ones would catch just as many flies? You know my pitch, Mikey. He's listening. He's watching me. That's what pastors do, I guess.

He asks me if I'm happier when I feel connected with God, and I tell him yes. What if Jesus made it easier for you to connect with God? he says. He says to accept, just for the sake of the argument, that maybe Jesus is the son of God. That would make him half divine and half human, he says. He could be a bridge between us and God. It would be like having an uncle in the furniture business when you need a new living room suite. I'm sure he's used that line in his sermons, Mikey.

I tell him accepting Jesus as the son of God is hard

for me. Mikey, you know I believe Jesus is a human em-
bodiment of God, but why does he have to be the only
one? What about the Buddha? What about Mother Te-
resa? That's what I ask the pastor. It seems so arbitrary
to me. God sacrificing his son is a spin-off on Abraham
sacrificing Isaac. Something to impress the Jews. And
they weren't even impressed! How can Pastor Ken not
be snowed by my biblical erudition, Mikey?

Look, he says. Jesus said he was the son of God. Either
he was lying, or he was crazy, or it was the truth. There
are no other options. That's exactly what he says to me,
Mikey. There are no other options. Two thousand years
later, millions and millions of people worship him. I'm
trying to remember exactly how he said it, Mikey. Are
they worshipping a nut case? A liar? Or is he the son of
God? It's a strong argument, Mikey.

He says Terry has told him I believe in the big bang
theory. He says he does, too. He asks if it's any crazier to
believe that all the unimaginable vastness of the universe
came from something the size of a bee's dick? That's what
he said, Mikey. A bee's dick. Not bad for a parson.

For some reason, it doesn't threaten you to believe in
the big bang theory, he says. But to believe in the divinity
of Christ? What would your friends think, right? He's getting to me, Mikey. What if Jesus truly is the only begotten
son of God, in some totally strange way we never can and
are not supposed to understand? Why is that any more bi-

zarre than the weird scientific crap you and I both believe in? Dick and crap, Mikey. This parson is OK.

He tells me try praying to Jesus and ask him to put in a word to his dad. He says the Bible is the revealed word of God, a handbook on how to live. Give it a shot, he says. Either it works or it doesn't. I remember saying stuff like that to you, Mikey.

But why would God create a son just to have him tortured to death, I ask him? We're all sinners, he says. That's why we feel vaguely guilty all the time. He says don't even bother trying to deny it. I wasn't going to, Mikey. He says God had Jesus born to die for our sins. For all the nasty stuff we do. If we can make a leap of faith and accept that he took the guilt for all our sins on his shoulders, we can feel forgiven and experience greater peace of mind than we ever thought possible.

He asks if I plan on visiting his little establishment again. I tell him I like the place. And Terry plays piano there. He asks me to keep an open mind about the Boy. I tell him I will. Suspend disbelief, he says. Have a conversation with Jesus. Ask him about the bible. Tell him it seems nuts to you, but you're willing to give it a shot. He says faith is the real source of strength and power. Not common sense. He says faith flies in the face of reason and facts. Facts change over time, he says. Ask Galileo and Newton and Einstein. Well, when you get to heaven you can ask them. That laugh again. Haw haw!

Terry is a truly special woman, he says. That's why I'm taking this time with you. I hope you don't mind. I tell him I'm honored, Mikey. He says he has to go. More old ladies with broken hips probably. We get up from the booth. He says don't worry about the coffee and the Bud. He runs a tab in the joint. Then he turns and walks out. I stand there for a while and then move out into the sun. It's only five o'clock. I drive home thinking, thinking, thinking. Why have I always been so resistant to religion and to Jesus? Now this woman is in my life who loves him so much. What does it mean? Belief in coincidence is a form of superstition. My old favorite saying.

I call Terry and tell her about my meeting with Pastor Ken. I know she'll be wondering how it went. The next day, we get together and go for a walk on the beach. I think about the time I watched someone getting baptized in the Delaware, where I used to swim when I was nine or ten. The other kids and I had laughed and pointed as some guy got dunked in the water, dodging, we thought, the boneless browns and Delaware whitefish.

That's what's happening in my life, kid. Write me what's happening in yours. Tell me what's happening with Kiera. Your job. Your life. I wanna know.

Keep going to meetings.

SENT: Friday, May 22, 1992 5:12 PM
To: mailformikey@aol.com
Subject: On the beach

Mikey, I went to the beach this morning. I've been going there every day. It's May and warm and the gulls are going nuts. There was actually a pair of pelicans there today. God knows where they flew in from but there they were, standing in the sand, looking out at the sea like two old Jewish men. "Whadaya think, Morris?" "I dunno. What could be? I dunno."

I stood there looking at the birds and found myself thinking about Jesus. Ever since my session with that pastor, I can't get my mind off God's kid. The one who paid me a visit. The one I've never offered enough respect to. What makes me such a hotshot that I have to question his divinity? And do I even question it anymore? There's a stubbornness in me that holds on to things just because I've gotten used to them. Over and over again, I ask myself what I really feel about him? Day after day on the beach, Mikey, my mind turns to whether or not he is God's actual kid. Such a weird strange concept. And so ridiculed by the elite.

The elite. Do I really need to suck up to them? Do I really give a damn what they think? The pseudo-intellectual snobs who don't have the guts to ask a question like what came before the big bang? They make fun of Christians for believing in miracles. Webster's definition of a miracle, Mikey, is something that goes against known scientific laws. Well, they claim matter and energy created itself out of nothing. That violates the first law of thermodynamics. They claim life popped up on its own out of non-life. That violates the law of biogenesis. So both sides believe in miracles. Why not go for the ones that make us happier?

If God had the power to take a pinpoint of energy and create the whole damn universe out of it, couldn't he have decided to make a kid with a human woman? Of course, he could. But why would he? Pastor Ken gave me a bunch of answers. But what do I think? What do I feel? Not just about Jesus, but about anything? What am I feeling right now I ask myself?

Stubborn, comes back the answer. No. Angry. I realize I'm really angry about something. But what, Mikey? Do I need a shrink? Should I lie down here on the beach and start analyzing my dreams? There's something I won't let go of, and it's standing in the way of the next big step in my life. I know it somehow. But what? I try to quiet the roof chatter in my head and figure out what's going on in there.

Screw 'em, I hear myself say in my mind. Screw who, I ask? Them! But who? I start howling inside. The bastards who took my *dog*! And there I am again, a twelve-year-old boy, hopelessly charging after that animal control van and screaming for Buster. And I realize that's what I won't give up, Mikey. That old hurt. I'm punishing myself to punish them. Like a little kid who goes out in the backyard to eat dirt. And if I don't let go of it, Terry will slip away. I'll lose her. I know it.

A terror takes me over. No. I can't let her go. I can't do this to myself. I fall on my knees in the sand. I don't care who's watching. Please God, I pray. Help me. I need help. I don't hear any answer, Mikey. I'm terrified. Is He abandoning me when I need Him most? Then Pastor Ken's words echo in my mind. Try praying to Jesus. Ask him to put in a word to his dad. Okay, Jesus, I say. I say it out loud. If you're there, if you're listening, I'm begging for your help. And I was begging, Mikey, from the deepest part of my soul: don't let me lose Terry like I lost Buster.

I suddenly see my mother and father in a different way. Not the cruel bullies from my childhood, but sad, frightened little people snapping at each other for lack of anything better to do. They probably were scared they'd get sued if Buster bit someone. A wave of forgiveness washes over me. Rest in peace wherever you are, I whisper, and I really mean it, Mikey. And at that moment of forgiveness, I have an image of God's kid, Jesus, with that half-smile on his face, and I hear him say come to me. And I do, Mikey. I let go in every part of me. I surrender.

Tears pour out of my eyes and down my cheeks. Tears of happiness. Oh hell, I say. Oh crap, oh shit. I am so damn happy. I am so lucky to be alive. Oh I love you, Jesus. Oh I love you, God. Oh I love you, Terry. Oh thank you, God, for this beautiful, beautiful world. Oh thank you. Thank you. Thank you. I can't say it enough.

The next thing that occurs to me is it might be nice if I cleaned up my language. It is God I'm speaking to, after all. It is Jesus. It is the Holy Spirit. Uh oh. I'm not even going there, Mikey. Understanding two out of three is enough for now. Alright, I say. I don't have to talk bad to prove I'm a macho guy. I start to laugh. Standing there on the beach, just laughing. I want to call Terry and tell her that me and Jesus have a good thing goin'. I feel a little sheepish about breaking the news to her. But I do love Jesus. I do love Terry. What's wrong with our having a nice little threesome?

I'm home and writing this before I make the call. To help me collect my thoughts. My mind is spinning. It's a major change in my life. Change? It's a transformation. I'll let you know. Love you, kid.

Keep going to meetings.

Santa Monica, CA
December 26, 1992

Dear Mikey,

It's a trip down Memory Lane writing to an APO address. Brings back all my years in the corps. I'm still reeling from the double whammy. I figured it was a matter of time till you eloped with that sweet girl, but your enlisting really caught me off guard. You phone to say you've joined up, you're leaving for boot camp the next day, and then for months I hardly get a penny postcard. Alright, don't apologize, I know what it's like. But it really made me realize how much I've come to love you, lad. The son I never had, etc. etc. Boo hoo. Forgive the mush. But I mean it.

When you showed up unannounced at my doorstep with your new wife on your arm, I almost lost it. You looked so great in your dress blues, and it was grand to see Kiera glowing like that. Terry got to meet her, at last. Wish your dad could see you. Well, wherever he is, he's proud. And God knows I am. You'll make a better Marine than I did. Then you announce you're only here for one night and shipping out the next day. And to Africa! Holy God. So, no more handy e-mailing. Out with the old Smith Corona, and here comes all the news. I don't know when you'll get this, but I'll keep writing to APO till I get a better address.

You got a chance to see how great everything looks while you were here. Like the Kennedys, we have a compound. It was all Marshall. Turns out he's some kind of a contractor. He got both houses painted inside and out, and he re-plumbed the one he'd been staying in. Even did the yard and put up the swing and slide set for little Aram. He was fine about having to move out. Knew he'd have to if they decided to come. When they did decide, he volunteered to hang on a while and supervise the re-do on the cheap. He moved into the little apartment over the garage. You remember I told you once you could crash there when you were afraid they were going to kick you out of your place for drunk and disorderly? It's great. Sitting room, small bedroom, bath and kitchenette.

Terry's mother and sister are staying there now while they're up here from Phoenix for Christmas. They're fine. I like them both well enough, and they seem to be OK with me. They're certainly pleasant. They probably wish she'd fallen for a younger guy. But she's forty, and she isn't married yet, so I guess they're settling for me. Her father is dead. They don't talk much about him, and neither does Terry. I know she loved him, but I guess it was complicated.

Carmen and company showed up two weeks ago. They stopped off in Boston and spent a few days with his people in Watertown. Then they flew on to LAX, and I picked them up on the 8th. Little Aram is adorable. He's almost two. He's got his father's Armenian honk and big sexy brown eyes and a mop of dark hair and a fabulous personality. He laughs all the time. And right off the bat, he bonded with Ralph. It reminds me of me and Buster. They wrestle on the grass, and it's hilarious. We stand there in the yard watching them and howl.

Vascan turns out to be a good guy. I've never really had a chance to get to know him. When we've been together, it's always been for a day or two here and there, and of course, I've wanted to spend most of the time with Carmen. They love the place. Carmen had sent me paint samples, and the house was done just the way she wanted. Their stuff arrived three weeks before <u>they</u> did. His new company paid to have it flown over. Do you believe it? A whole houseful of furniture? It shows you how much they want him. I sent her a plan of the place. Marshall drew it up for me. So she pencils in where the furniture should go and mails it back, and when the moving guys deliver the stuff, I stand there like a traffic cop. This goes here. That goes there. All she had to do was unpack the boxes of blankets and can openers.

I've been going to meetings, of course. Spending time with Terry. Crazy about her. Going to church. Yes, yes. Don't laugh. Every Sunday. Alright, what do you want from me. Carmen thinks I'm nuts too. She says papa, your whole life you've been an addict. Booze, cigarettes, women, God knows what. Now you're addicted to Jesus. Maybe she's right, I don't know. I don't understand it. I've given up trying. My life is so much better now. That's all I know. And now that it is, an idea starts bopping around in my head, Mikey.

The Lutherans aren't heavy on being born again. But every other Sunday these days, Ken seems to come back to John the Baptist dunking Jesus in the Jordan. So, here we are ten minutes away from the grand and glorious Pacific Ocean. And I start to get obsessed with the idea of making a whole new start. Of being reborn. Of course, I was baptized when I was a baby. Why they did it, I don't know. I had no idea it was happening. And my parents never even went to church or, as far as I could see, gave a damn about whether God existed or not.

Anyway, one Sunday a few months ago, Terry and I are walking out of the chapel. So I tell her what I've been thinking about. She goes nuts and makes me turn right around and tell Pastor Ken before he leaves. Which we do, and he laughs and says you're a fast worker. He says maybe in a week or two, he'll set up a baptism ceremony as part of a regular Sunday service. I tell him what I'd like is to go down to the beach with him and Terry and have him dunk me under the water the way John the Baptist did Jesus. He looks at me a minute, and then he says Ok, that would be alright. When would you like to do it? Tomorrow at four I say.

He starts to laugh. Haw haw haw. Alright, he says. Terry gets off work at three thirty. Don't you? She says she does. So, we'll meet here, and I'll drive us to the parking lot at the pier. He gives me a fellow-Christian hug and goes back into the church. Terry gives me the kind of hug I really like, and I walk her home.

The next day, I'm a wreck, Mikey, on account of my date to get born again. What's it going to feel like? How am I going to feel afterward? When it gets close to the time, I put on my blue swimming trunks and my sandals and a nice white Mexican shirt I never wear. I grab a couple of beach towels and head out the door. When I get to the playground behind the church, most of the kids are already gone. There are just a couple climbing on the Jungle Gym. At quarter of four, Terry comes out of her classroom with a really sweet white dress on. Are you coming in the water with us, I ask her? I certainly am, she says, and I'm wearing this dress. She looks at me in my swimming trunks. Nice legs, she says.

At five to four, Pastor Ken comes out of his office. He looks at my swimming trunks and says nice legs. We get in his car. It's an old Dodge Dart. I'm lugging the beach towels. Pastor Ken has a bible and a towel of his own. He says he's got a bathing suit on under his pants. Terry hops in the back, and the two of us guys are up front. Do we have to get a permit for this, I ask him. Is it legal? We won't ask, he says. I reach back and take Terry's hand. I'm nervous.

We get to the pier and drive out on it. It's pretty empty. A cloudy Monday afternoon. Good, I think. I make a little prayer in my head. Please Lord, help me do this right. We park the Dart and go down the wooden steps to the sand. There's a few teenagers with surfboards at the edge of the water. I try to steer us away from them without looking too obvious about it.

We come to a dry spot near where the beach starts to get damp. Pastor Ken spreads his towel out. He says let's sit here for a minute. I'd like to read you a passage from the good book. We all plunk down. Terry holds my hand. Ken leafs through his bible and finds the chapter he's looking for. He tells us it's from Mark. "And it came to pass that Jesus came from Nazareth, and was baptized by John in the Jordan and the Spirit descended upon Him like a dove. And a voice came from heaven, You are my beloved Son in whom I am well pleased." Pastor Ken closes his bible. He talks to us a little more about the meaning of baptism, and then he stands up.

Alright, into the drink we go he says. He drops his pants. He has on bright red swimming trunks. He sees us looking at them, and he blushes. The only ones I own, he says. We laugh and tell him it's fine. I kick off my sandals. Terry and Ken kick off theirs. My towels are in a little pile. Ken drops his bible on it. We head toward the ocean. I look around. No one's watching us. We wade on in. It's chilly. Terry holds her dress up till the water reaches her waist. Then she lets it float. Ken stops.

This is good, he says. He looks at me. I'm very proud to be doing this, he says. He puts one hand on my shoulder and the other on top of my head. I baptize you in the name of the father and of the son and of the holy spirit. He pushes me down and under the water. Then he pulls me up right away. I'm sopping wet and laughing. Congratulations, he says. Terry gives me a big squishy hug. Then she hugs Pastor Ken. How do you feel, she asks me? Reborn, I say. We all laugh, including me. But I mean it, I say.

Back on the beach, we dry ourselves off as best we can. Darn, says Terry, I forgot to bring a camera. So did I, says Ken. I tell them so what, it's engraved in my mind. Pastor Ken drives us back to church. I ask if we can buy him a beer, but he begs off. My wife sees little enough of me as it is. I thank him a lot, and he walks into the church. I look at Terry. You're saturated, I say. She says she's going home to change, and then let's have dinner and celebrate. And that's what we did, Mikey.

If you're wondering, I feel different since my dip in the sea. Really different. I'm not sure how to describe the feeling. I can see why they call it born again. It's like a fresh breeze blowing through me. I feel like Jesus is my friend, like we've made a bond.

So that's what I've been doing for the six months you've been learning to be a Marine, Mikey. Six months which I know was hell. Remember, I went through it, too. I imagine Kiera has told you we invited her up her for the holiday. She's been staying with Terry for a few days, and they really seem to have hit it off like sisters. Nothing could please me more. God knows she'll need some friends, not having much of any family. The life of a military wife is no stroll on the boardwalk.

On Christmas morning, Aram got everybody up at the crack of dawn to look in his stocking. They called me, and I ran next door. Such fun, Mikey. Look what Thanta brought! His funny little lisp. We did the main presents that afternoon. The night before, Terry and I had gone to a candlelight service at church. Christmas carols and families with kids. It was beautiful. Then we came back to my place late, and she tells me she wants us to exchange our gifts right then on Christmas Eve.

I'd found a little necklace for her. A plain gold chain with a simple crucifix fused onto a two-thousand-year-old Roman coin, Mikey. It was minted when the Empire was occupying the Holy Land. She loved it. Then she hands me my present. It's a Brooks Brothers box and in it is a fine gray cashmere V-neck pullover. Just the kind I like. I give her a hug and thank her. Then I pull the sweater from the box and an envelope drops out of it.

I open it and take out a plain white card with a single word written on it. Yes. It takes a second for it to sink in, and then my heart jumps, Mikey.

I grab her and hug her to me so hard I'm afraid she's going to crack. Oh God, I say. I love you so. And I'm dying to make love to you. She says I'm dying to have you make love to me. If you carried me up to your bed right now, I'm afraid I wouldn't be able to say no. I look in her eyes. But God wants us to wait. Right? She says nothing, but I can see the answer in her face. I grumble. I'm not waiting for you to be a June bride. What about a January wedding? She laughs. Give me a little time. I need to find a dress and print up invitations and all the rest of it. February then, I say. March, she says. Alright, but early March.

I went to Barnes and Noble and picked up an atlas and a book on Africa to try and find out something about where you said they were sending you. Somalia. Mogadishu. Doesn't sound like quite the placid place I'd imagined. Well, at least you're avoiding the hot spots like Beirut. You'll probably be teaching the locals how to dig wells or something. Maybe get to see some giraffes. Hang in there, kiddo. If you can't find a meeting, start one. Love you.

Santa Monica, CA
March 10, 1993

Dear Mikey,

Hey, kiddo. I'm still writing care of APO, not having anything else. Please write as soon as you can with something better. Terry and I rode the train down to S. D. and took Kiera out to dinner the other night. Nice little Italian joint. She looks great. Misses you terribly, of course, but seems to be holding up well. We call her a lot.

Here in the compound all goes well. Vascan has started work on his new job. Unfortunately, the company headquarters is all the way downtown, so he has a hell of a commute. But so be it. Carmen and Terry have hit it off fabulously. They're closer in age to each other than Terry is to me, really. I love to hear them chatting and laughing together over a glass of wine. Neither of them, incidentally, feels awkward about drinking around me, and I'm relaxed about it, too.

I've started taking Aram on walks with Ralph, and he loves it. Walk, walk, he'll say. Ralph hears it and gets all excited. Runs and picks up his leash from the chair by the front door. I feel there's a healing taking place inside me about Buster and my parents and me. A second chance to have things OK about a dog. I still take Ralph two or three times a week to the early morning dog run on the beach. It's his favorite thing in the world. Aram doesn't get up early enough yet to be able to go with us. I've run into Barry from church a few times with his dog, and the two mutts go at it like professional wrestlers.

The whole church knows about our wedding plans, of course, and they're all excited. She's such a fave there. We've decided to have the ceremony here in the compound. If we had it in church, we'd have to invite everybody, which we just can't do. And Terry doesn't want any hurt feelings. As it is, there'll be about a 125 people, with her church folks and my program people and her mom and sister and a couple of cousins. I don't have any family. Pastor Ken is OK about performing the wedding in the yard. The weather is iffy at this time of year, late March. We'll have a standby rent-a-tent if needed.

Terry is so excited. It's her first and only marriage, and she carries on and on about the dress, the invitations and everything surrounding the event. Her sister, two of her pals from church and Kiera are going to be the bridesmaids. Nice. Since I don't have you here to be best man, it's a toss up between Marshall and Vascan. I'm getting to know Vascan better and find him to be a guy of real substance. Carmen is lucky to have him. I'll let you know when I decide. Wish it could be you, pal.

I'll sign off now and write again soon care of APO. Please let me know a better address as soon as you can.

Love you, pal.

Santa Monica, CA
March 15, 1993

Dear Mikey,

Still no word from you, but I know it takes time for the corps to get these things set up. Kiera has told us the fabulous news, which I certainly hope you know. I can't believe it. A little Mikey on the way. Or a little Michelle. Or whoever. We suggested to her that when her time comes, she come up here and move into the apartment over the garage, and she said she'll think about it. I hope she agrees. She'll need help, and between Terry and Carmen, there'll be lots of help to give. Anyway, mucho congrats, dad.

The wedding is almost upon us. Pastor Ken worked a deal with the Broken Drum to cater the affair. Meatloaf, mashed potatoes and creamed spinach. An odd menu maybe, but easy to prepare and keep hot, and they do it well there. We'll have champers for the drinkers and Martinelli's Cider for the sober crowd. We got the invites from the printer, and they look good. A bit formal for my taste, but Terry gets the say-so about everything as far as I'm concerned. She's got a dress picked out, but of course, I won't see it till she comes walking down the aisle. She's thrilled, and that's what counts.

Aram keeps growing and talking a blue streak. An early talker, the experts say. Who knows? Experts are the ones who brought us Viet Nam and don't fix the potholes. I'm going to a couple of new meetings, which I'm getting a lot out of. A kid asked me to sponsor him, but with all that's happening, I said no and found him someone else. I hope you're still able to get meetings together in your outfit. Can't wait to hear about Somalia. There are pieces here and there in the Times, but nothing major. I suppose no news is good news.

Terry, Carmen and Vascan send their best. So does Ralph.

Love you, pal.

Santa Monica, CA
April 12, 1993

Huzzah!

At last a letter from you! Unfortunately, it came while we were away. On our HONEYMOON! Talk about happiness. Word from you that you're OK, and word from God that our whole new life together is off to a great start. Glad you're thrilled about Kiera's news, dad. You'll make a great father when you get to be home. Make sure that happens by BEING CAREFUL. It sounds pretty hairy over there. Who knew? I thought you were being sent to some quaint little National Geographic country.

OK, our news. Don't let anyone ever tell you that religious Christian women are not hot. Holy God! I'm wiped out. But a smile seems to be permanently engraved on my face. I'm going to invest in an aluminum walker, as I know I'll need one by the time she's through with me.

Our wedding was fabulous. The weather was so good for the two weeks leading up to the day that we cancelled the standby tent and saved the dough. We wound up with almost a hundred and fifty guests. There was a dance floor in the yard and a D.J. who played fabulous R and B and all kinds of other stuff including disco far into the night. We strung hundreds of Christmas tree-sized white lights overhead. It turns out Terry has a cousin or something on her dead father's side who heard about the wedding and offered to send them. He's in the light fixture business. So we invited him to the wedding, and he turned out to be a great new relative for Terry and a connection to her dad, which pleased her. The mom and sister were coolly polite to him is all. Maybe someday I'll find out what the story is.

Broken Drum sent waiters and hot trays and the food and drink. The tables and silver and tablecloths and plates and the dance floor we rented from a party outfit. The wedding began at four o'clock with chairs set up all over the place and Pastor Ken up on the porch. The head of our church band, a sweet, talented guitarist and singer name of Scotty, played and sang a song Terry picked. A James Taylor number about a river. That's what we all marched in to.

I hadn't seen her since the night before when we had a small rehearsal dinner at the English Pub. She went home after dinner and spent the evening with her mom and sis. Then on the day of the wedding, it's all about getting into the dress and laughing and carrying on with her family and the bridesmaids. The best-looking one was Kiera, I'm not just saying that, Mikey. At the start of the ceremony, Vascan and I are up on the porch with Pastor Ken. Then, Kiera and the sister and the other bridesmaids come out the door of Carmen's house followed by the mother and then Terry. When she comes out and walks down the aisle between the guests, I'm telling you I've never seen anyone so beautiful in my life.

Her hair is combed back with clips on either side and has a little crown of flowers in it. Her wedding dress is gorgeous. White silk, formfitting above the waist and the skirt longer in the back than in the front. She's wearing that cross on the coin that I gave her for Christmas, and she's carrying a little bouquet of daisies. I get tears in my eyes, Mikey. Vascan is best man and hands me the ring. We've got quite close in the few months since Christmas, and anyway, Marshall seems to have disappeared. I hope he hasn't "gone out," Mikey. Little Aram is supposed to march in the procession, but gets shy at the last minute and backs off.

Pastor Ken gives a talk about the sanctity of marriage. He can't resist getting a few laughs, of course. Then he asks if anyone knows any reason we shouldn't get hitched. I'm afraid one of our guys will yell out, yeah, he's a drunk! But they hold it in and Ken goes on, finishing with I now pronounce you husband and wife, you may kiss the bride. Cheers and yells, Mikey. We head into the house to take some photos. Phil Hughes from the morning meeting in Culver City has the job. He's a good photographer.

When we get to the top of the stairs, all the women, mostly from the church, gather on the grass, and Terry tosses the bouquet over her shoulder. Some hefty dame that everybody likes catches it, and there's a big laugh and applause. We take the pictures inside. Terry asks her dad's cousin to be in them, which pleases him a lot. The mom and sis seem OK about it, as everyone is so happy by this time, nothing can spoil the mood. While Terry's changing out of her wedding gown, the caterers are moving the chairs and setting up the dinner tables. When that's going on, everyone is over at one side of the yard drinking champagne or Martinelli's. There are a few guys there that you'd know, Mikey, and they ask about you.

After a while, we all come out and the guests sit down at the tables. It's getting chilly by that time, but we have those portable gas heaters in between every other table, and they get lit, so soon enough the air is cozy. There's some kind of a salad to start with that Terry picked out. I don't care about salad, but the women have to have it. Then they serve the meat loaf and mashed potatoes, which some people seem to find funny when it shows up, but to hell with them. After they taste it, though, they all seem to be happy. There's plenty of it, and a lot of people ask for seconds. You can never go wrong with meat loaf if it's good, Mikey.

Then there's the wedding cake, and Terry and I have to get up and cut while Phil Hughes snaps more pictures. After the cake, there's toasts. Nice ones from the church crowd and jokes about my being too old and passing out on the wedding night from the program guys. All good-natured stuff. Terry and I have the first dance, then everybody joins in, and the night goes on until about eleven when the cops show up. Somebody has complained about the noise. So we invite the cops in and tell the D.J. to turn the volume down.

Around eleven thirty, Terry and I sneak out and drive to the Sheraton in Marina del Rey, where I've made a reservation for the night. Bliss, Mikey, bliss. You know how good dinner tastes when you haven't eaten a bunch of hors d'oeuvres first? Need I say more? In the morning, we pop back home to pick up our suitcases, which we've pre-packed for the trip. We hug everybody goodbye, Aram cries because he can't go with us, but we tell him we'll bring him a present, and that does the trick. Terry's mother cries, and everyone wishes us bon voyage, and we're off to Mazatlan and a fabulous week. It corresponds with spring vacation at Terry's school, so the timing is perfect.

My fingers are getting tired on the typewriter, Mikey, so I'm going to sign off. I'm so glad you're alive and well, though it seems life is nerve-wracking for you over there. I promise we'll keep an eye on Kiera. She seems to be doing fine, not much morning sickness. Write again soon.

Watch your tail, lad. Best from all of us. Keep going to meetings.

Love you, pal.

Santa Monica, CA
June 22, 1993

Wow Mikey!

It's fertility heaven around here. Maybe the other girls were jealous of Kiera. Carmen is pregnant again, and, Praise the Lord, so is Terry. Nine weeks to the day after we got married! We can't believe it. Carmen's was out of the blue, though she's not unhappy about it at all. Terry's been trying like crazy, as my aching back and permanent smile will testify to. We've talked about it a lot, of course. It wasn't my first choice. At my age, I'd have preferred to have her all to myself, to be able to take trips and be free to be a couple. And I have a kid and a grandkid. But I wasn't going to say no to her. I think every woman wants and needs to experience motherhood if she can. And if you could see how happy she looks.

When she thought there was a chance she might be preggers, she went to the Thrifty and picked up one of those kits that tell you yes or no. I think the Save the Rabbit League financed the invention of those. Well, it turned purple or whatever it's supposed to do. She went nuts, but went back and bought another one to make sure. But she's forty-one, and it's tricky. She ran to her doctor, I don't remember what they call those docs, not an obstetrician, but whatever. The doc is a dame, and Terry says she's great. She told her to eat lots of protein, rest as much as possible, all the usual stuff. Well, Carmen and Terry are hugging each other, and they call Kiera, who's thrilled for them, and they arrange for her to come up and meet them for lunch and eat their salad or whatever the hell it is dames do at lunch. Aram doesn't know yet he's going to have a little brother or sister. Carmen will tell him when the time is right. She's a great mother, and Terry is lucky to have her so close.

So you and I are both going to be daddies. Bless your heart, lad. Hang in there and write when you can. I try to follow the news, but Somalia is not high on the top ten list of subjects for feature stories.

Love you, pal.

Santa Monica, CA
August 17, 1993

Yo Mikey,

No news from you, sad new from us. Terry lost the baby. She was in her third month. That's the dangerous time, the doc says. When a woman gets to be in her forties, her eggs have been in cold storage all those years, and their chances of staying stuck to the walls of the uterus are way less than when she was younger. Miscarriage is also called spontaneous abortion. It's God's way of keeping a deformed kid from getting born. When you see a mongoloid baby, its mother is almost always older. I remember giving you a whole lecture on this subject, Mikey.

So, that's that. She says she wants to try again, so away we go. It really is in God's hands. But meanwhile, she's in my hands, and that's alright. Your girl's pregnancy is going great guns, and so is Carmen's. That must be hard on Terry, but she prays and says she's fine and is very loving to the other two women. She's also becoming like a second mother to little Aram. Teree, Teree, he yells when he sees her. She's been taking him to the playground in the park.

Summer is almost over, not that you'd know it out here, but it means school starts up, and she'll be going back to work. I hold her in bed a lot at night and let her cry. Then she gets horny. Ah, the joys of married life.

Kiera gets up here a lot, or we go see her. She's really showing. Showing and glowing. But I know it's hard on her to hear from you so rarely. Try and write to her more, kiddo. She needs it. Even if the news is bad, it's better than no news. This will be a quick note as I'm off to a new meeting, don't want to be late and need to post this in the box.

Love you, kiddo.

Santa Monica, CA
October 5, 1993

Oh Jesus, kid:

I don't even know if you're going to be able to read this. I'm sending it to the hospital in Germany where they've taken you. It's all over the news. All those soldiers gone. You had to be one of the handful of Marines attached to the force. We're praying for you morning, noon and night. Kiera has come up and moved into the little apartment and is staying here with us where she needs to be. She cries and cries. We wait for info every minute. When the bell rings on the gate, we dread the sight of Marines bearing bad news. They say you're in a medically induced coma, so they can work on you. They don't know if you'll wake up or not. Oh God, kid, how can we bear it. How can Kiera bear it. We ask Jesus for help to get through it and to accept God's will in this matter as in all things. How many times do I remember you throwing that advice back at me, Mikey.

We're taking care of Kiera and will do so as long as she needs us to. She's due in two months. Your son will

be called Mikey Jr. She actually plans to have him christened Mikey, not Michael. That's how she knows and
loves you she says. Pastor Ken comes to visit. Terry's pregnant again and keeping a stiff upper lip, but we know
the chances aren't good. Carmen is so very loving and
helpful both to Kiera and Terry. Little Aram knows nothing, of course. Ralph doesn't get to the beach as often as
he'd like with all that's going on. The church people are
sweet and helpful, but the truth is, almost nothing helps
but faith and prayer.

Hang in there, kid.

Santa Monica, CA
November 2, 1993

Dear Mikey,

Your beautiful son was born at 6:12 a.m. this morning at St. John's Hospital. Kiera is doing fine. Terry and Carmen were in the delivery room with her and watched Mikey Jr. come out and look around as if to say, Where's my dad?! He's seven pounds plus, I don't remember the exact ounces, but wanted to get this letter off to you so that when, not if, you wake up, you won't have to wait for the good news.

Vascan and I were just outside the delivery area and were able to see him when he was twenty-five minutes old. What a kid! You'd be so proud if you could be here, lad. As we're all so proud of you. We pray in shifts, and the whole church has you on something they call a prayer chain. They've done blind studies on the power of prayer, Mikey. Even people who don't know they're being prayed for are helped. Of course, as I used to remind you and as you have on more than one occasion reminded me, it's all in God's hands. The doctors have not given up hope, and for sure, we haven't. You are loved so very much, kid.

I'll sign off and get this in the mail. I'm going on a pizza run and will be bringing a fine big sausage and green pepper pie up to room 317 at St. John's.

Don't give up the ship, We have only begun to fight. The only thing we have to fear is fear itself. We shall fight them on the beaches!

Love you, kiddo

Santa Monica, CA
May 12, 2008

Dear Mikey,

If you had made it, lad, you wouldn't recognize the world today. Since 9-11, it's all so different in this country. Cell phones and they can say anything they want on TV, and the movie theaters all have stadium seating. But some things stay the same, and I thought I'd write you this letter on what would have been the seventeenth anniversary of your sobriety. Terry is going to walk down to the ocean with me near where I got baptized. I'll read it aloud to her, and I think in some way you'll be listening along with her.

Mikey Jr. is a young man of fourteen now. Gorgeous. That is to say, he looks like you. Kiera sent us a picture of him. She stayed with us for a year, and Terry helped mother your baby. It broke her heart when Kiera took him and moved away, but it was time. A few years after that, she met and married a really sweet guy who loves her and has adopted Mikey and is raising him. But he keeps your picture on the wall of his bedroom and is proud that you are his dad, Kiera says. She lives in Cleveland now, and we hear from her once in a while.

Carmen had a little girl and named her Gloria. She's fourteen now too and simply adorable. When Terry lost our second child, which was very hard for her because she had kept it for almost four months, she accepted her lot and has become a second mother to Aram and Gloria. I can see how much they love her and how good it is for them to have this expanded family. They are in and out of both houses all the time, raiding our cookie jar and asking Terry for help with homework.

Actually, both kids wound up going to the Lutheran school where Terry teaches, though neither Carmen nor Vascan are believers. Some of it rubbed off on Aram. He went to church with us and Sunday school. When he was six, he came home and said to his father, "Dad, did you know Jesus is king?" Poor Vascan. Gloria is thrillingly beautiful. She has Carmen's nose, thank God, and her Latin complexion and her father's sexy Armenian eyes. She's a fabulous artist and spends afternoons in our house drawing at the kitchen table. Vascan's job lasted two years, and then his hotshot company went broke. He went through a really lean period for a while, but hung in there and is now doing fabulously well again. He's like a son to me. The Armenian relatives come to visit about once a year and stay in the little apartment. They are crazy as outhouse rats, but loveable.

I'm so in love with my wife. What a gift from God. I'm getting to be a bit of an alter cocker, but we still make love from time to time. She says she plans on giving up teaching, but I'll believe it when I see it. Each new generation of schoolkids adores her. So do Aram and Gloria. No children of her own, but surrounded by other people's kids who love her.

I'm so blessed, Mikey. Everything changes when you let Jesus into your life. Everything. Each new day is a miracle. I'm constantly filled with gratitude. I've sponsored a few young guys over the years. Good for me and I hope good for them. So that's my news, Mikey. Oh, Ralph the dog lasted a long time and then passed away at the foot of our bed. We buried him in the yard. Sooner or later, I suppose God will send me another dog. I miss you so very much, kid. When I think back on all the stuff I made you listen to. Probably just so I could hear it myself. What an odyssey we went through together.

Well, I'll be seeing you. I know Terry worries about what she'll do after I'm gone, but I keep telling her that won't be for a long time. One night when Carmen and Vascan were going out, and Aram had a sleepover at a friend's house, we were baby-sitting little Gloria at our place. I guess she was five or six. When it was time for her to go to bed in our guest room, she started to cry and said she felt alone and scared. There's a wooden chair in the corner. I moved it next to the bed and told her this chair is where Jesus sits, and she'll never be alone as long as it's there and he's in it. She stopped crying and seemed comforted. When the time does come for me to leave Terry, I'll put that chair next to her bed and tell her she'll never be alone.

Meanwhile, Mikey, say hello to Jesus for me. Tell him if you saw any majestic elephant shtupps when you were in Africa.

Love you, pal.

ACKNOWLEDGMENTS

Many thanks to my wonderful family, especially my son-in-law, Marc Atlan, for designing the wonderful book jacket; my son-in-law, Andrew Breitbart, for so generously helping to get the book promoted; and my son, Max Bean, for his invaluable aid in teaching me the mysteries of putting this book together on the computer. A special thank you to my friend Dean Koontz, who essentially functioned as my editor. And many thanks to my friend David Blasband for sending the manuscript to sweet Carole Stuart at Barricade Books. Many thanks to Richard Dry and Flavia Colgan for editorial help, and to George Carlin, Bernie Goldberg, Pastor Ken Frese, Nancy Perkins, Tom Williams, Janet and Mark Sweeney, Ralph Prey, Margot Atwell, and finally, Gerald Schroeder, who lives in Israel and who I've never met, but whose amazing book, *The Hidden Face of God*, taught me so much.

ORSON BEAN's career spans over five decades, from the Golden Age of television in the fifties ("Playhouse Ninety," "The Twilight Zone") to a six-year run on "Dr. Quinn, Medicine Woman" in the nineties to his SAG Award-nominated performance in *Being John Malkovich*. In addition to being an actor and director, he is a storyteller and raconteur who sat on the panel of the game show "To Tell the Truth" for seven years and guested on "The Tonight Show" over two hundred times (one hundred of them as guest host).

He starred on Broadway for twenty years, enjoying long runs in such plays as *Never Too Late* and *Will Success Spoil Rock Hunter* and in a number of musicals including

175

Subways Are for Sleeping, for which he received a Tony Award nomination. His numerous film credits include *Anatomy of a Murder*, *Innerspace* and *Forty Deuce*. Three new independent pictures in which he appears await release this year.

Bean works frequently on television, guesting on dramas like "Cold Case," "Women's Murder Club" and "The Closer" as well as on sitcoms such as "Two and a Half Men" and "How I Met Your Mother."

A successful author, he has had three books published: *Me and the Orgone*, which recounts his experience in Reichian therapy, *Too Much Is Not Enough*, an autobiography, and the satirical *25 Ways to Cook a Mouse*. Born in Burlington, Vermont (and second cousin to Calvin Coolidge), he survived the industry blacklist of the 1950s. He currently lives in Venice, California, with his wife, the actress Alley Mills, where they are both members of the acclaimed Pacific Resident Theater. He has four children and seven grandchildren. He is one lucky son of a bitch.